I0469801

Labyrinth Breaker

The Next Generation of Space War
Sci-Fi MOVIE SCRIPT

RAGHAVENDRA RATHORE
RAMENDRA RATHOR

Copyright © 2019 by Raghavendra Rathore and Ramendra Rathor
All rights reserved. No part of this book may be used or reproduced by any
means, graphic, electronic, or mechanical, including photocopying,
recording, taping, or by any information storage retrieval system, without
the written permission of the publisher except in the case of brief
quotations embodied in critical articles and reviews.

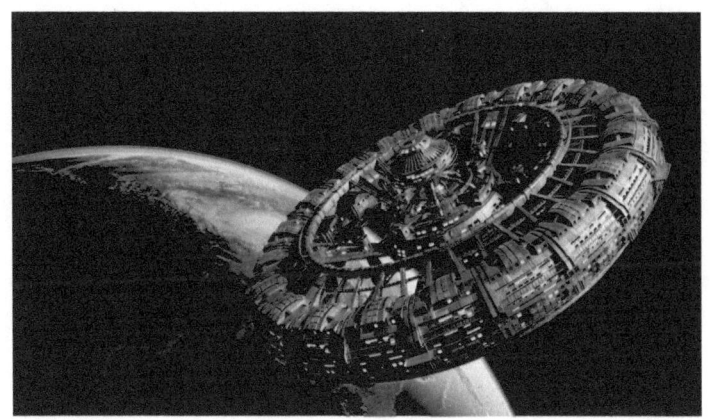

Table of Contents

Name of characters

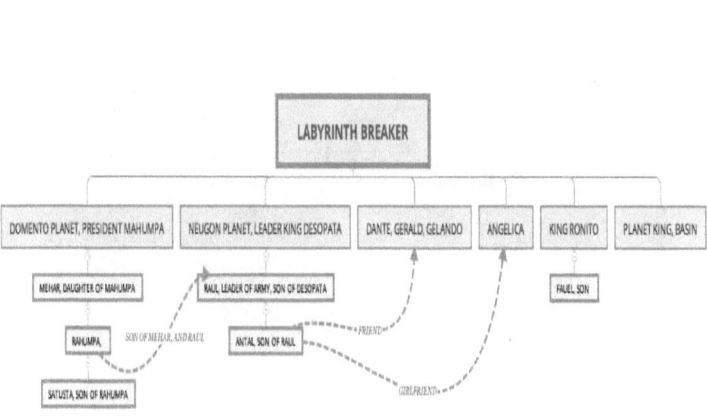

LABYRINTH BREAKER

| DOMENTO PLANET, PRESIDENT MAHUMPA | NEUGON PLANET, LEADER KING DESOPATA | DANTE, GERALD, GELANDO | ANGELICA | KING RONITO | PLANET KING, BASIN |

MEHAR, DAUGHTER OF MAHUMPA

RAUL, LEADER OF ARMY, SON OF DESOPATA

FAUEL, SON

RAHUMPA,   SON OF MEHAR, AND RAUL

ANTAL, SON OF RAUL   « FRIEND »

SATUSTA, SON OF RAHUMPA   « GIRLFRIEND »

Acknowledgments

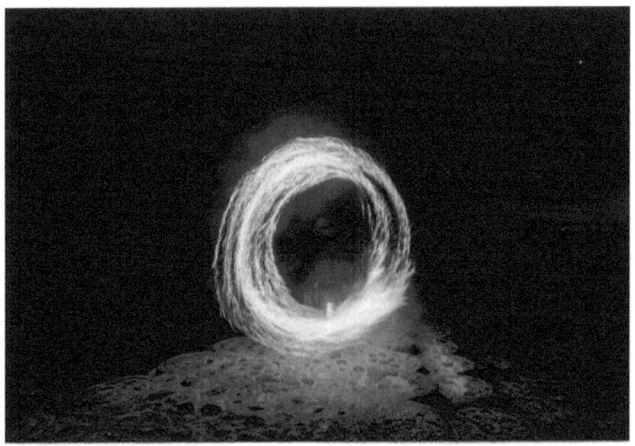

This book is possible because my family has inspired me every day to write something that explains Story in a way that makes it easy and understandable for you, the reader, and those who inspired me to write it.

Moreover, thank you to the friends and students whose questions and comments over the years have helped me more fully understand what those aspiring to learn more about movie script will need to know more before they get into more complex aspects and lessons.

Introduction

When Rahumpa escalates a labyrinth space war, nobody can win. It all started when his grandfather Mahumpa, the leader of the planet Domento, decided to take control of the planet Neugon. After a lot of effort and many years with no success, he devises a plan for defeating the Neugons, who have a scientist, named Raul that creates high-tech machines. Meher seduces Raul, and her and Raul's DNA are used to create a super-child, who she names Rahumpa.

When Rahumpa gets older and takes up his grandfather's mantle, the tables turn, and he destroys and controls all the nearby planets, taking hold with an unbeatable army.

Meanwhile, Raul moves forward, with no knowledge that Rahumpa is his son, and has a son named Antal, who eventually becomes the leader of the Neugons. Antal declares that they win the war against Rahumpa and enlists the smartest people in the universe to work together.

To win this war, he must break the chains forged by his half-brother, struggling through the labyrinth of advanced technology and medicine. Antal is unlike Raul and Mahumpa—he believes in peace and has a brave heart. One day, while protecting another world's labs and scientists, he falls in love with the president's daughter, Angelica, who is a renowned expert with guns.

Rahumpa made a big mistake, though: he kidnaps Angelica when she doesn't have any of her firearms handy and wants to force her to marry him. While holding her hostage, he designs and creates a set of spaceships that work together in a series of circles, with only one way in and out. The end of the war leads to Antal and Rahumpa learning that they are brothers. Will Antal ever win the war, or will Rahumpa always be unbeatable?

The lead character in this movie script is Mahumpa, the leader of the planet Domento, and his daughter Meher. Rahumpa, the son of Meher and Raul, takes over for Mahumpa as leader. Raul's other son, Antal, becomes the leader of the planet Neugon and takes over as the main protagonist. Antal's girlfriend Angelica and friends Dante, Gelando, Gerald, and

King Bashin will help Antal in this epic space war, the Labyrinth Breaker.

Labyrinth Breaker

THE SCREENPLAY

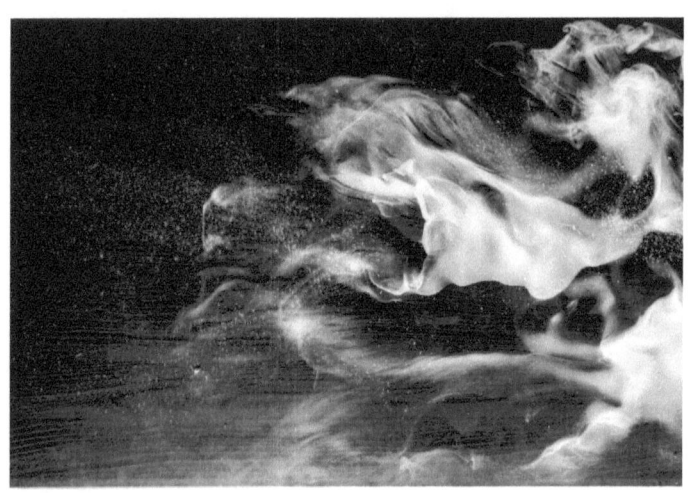

Ext. Highly smoky and cloudy

The sky is cloaked in clouds, heavy smoke filling the air. The sounds of blasters firing could be heard all around, with flashes of lights visible in the clouds, but not from lightning.

The Domento planet armed forces, clad in pristine black uniforms, remotely launch a hefty piece of machinery from the grips of four planes.

It starts spinning in the sky, coming down to the base of the Neugon army, distinct in their blue and white uniforms, and enters their invisible shield.

The machine that looked so dangerous in the air stops and falls to the ground.

One soldier runs and changes a chip tray in the machine, then runs back.

A different person from the Neugon army triggers a, button with a computer and machine lights turning on and starting to spin and shoot into the sky. Missiles fire from the machine against the same army that dropped it. It fires the missiles and laser beams from multiple angles, leaving a swath of destruction of the army in black. All the fighter planes commanded by the Domento army come around to destroy their machine with missiles of their own.

CUT TO:

Int. In a computer lab

A hand triggers a red button.

FADE TO:

Ext. Battlefield

The deadly machine, airplanes, and other war machines explode.

FADE IN:

Int. Meeting hall

A man named MAHUMPA (President of Domento planet) sits in a meeting hall, tensely clutching a remote as he watches a live telecast of the war, with crystal-clear 3-D images that display more detail than he can bear to watch.

MAHUMPA

Why am I hearing bad news from all over?

His anger is met with silence. He glances at the flag in the corner, to remind himself what he is fighting for.

He sighs, and then punches the table, and the 3-D images disappear.

The other people in the meeting stand up, shoving their chairs back, waiting to see what their leader would say next.

MAHUMPA

Is this how we have designed war?

The woman to his right, her silver hair spun into a perfectly tight bun, stands up. Her voice is quiet, but unwavering.

WOMAN (ADVISER)

President MAHUMPA, we simply don't know how they got this advanced technology. Someone was able to take command of one of their weapons, but they didn't know how to operate it.

MAHUMPA

(gritting teeth)

Another defeat. We have no chance of winning this war.

No one speaks up, keeping his or her heads down. MAHUMPA looks at them and takes a deep breath.

MAHUMPA

(voice cracking)

Get my army back here and let me know where the Neugons are getting their technology from. I want to know precisely who is providing it to them. And I need to know this now.

MAHUMPA slams his fist on the table to emphasize his point before standing up and heading out through the door.

A general Thomas, looking sharp in his uniform and dignified with every gray hair in perfect place, of the army strides up to the end of the hallway, two well-dressed young men (MIKE and LARRY) following close behind him.

The general presses a button on the wall, and a screen lights up on the door as the hallway opens to allow him inside.

MAHUMPA stands up and gestures to the general, ignoring the men behind him.

MAHUMPA

Come on in, General Thomas. The door is open.

The three newest people stand at the front, arms behind their backs.

THOMAS

President MAHUMPA, I have some news for you. I would like to introduce you to MIKE and LARRY, who have been spying on the enemy base for the last six months.

MAHUMPA turns toward MIKE and LARRY.

MAHUMPA

What information do we have?

LARRY

We know who is behind all of this.

MIKE pulls out what looks like a pen and presses the button on it. A projected screen shows up with a man's image on the wall.

MIKE

This is the only person behind the technology of the Neugons. They call him a super-genius.

LARRY

Without their technology, their army is structurally weak. From the invisible shield to the speed of their fighter jets, their strength relies on their tech. No tech means no Neugons.

MAHUMPA grins and shakes LARRY's hand, then MIKE's.

MAHUMPA

Thank you for your hard work. What should we do now? Can we get him to join us?

LARRY

I'm afraid not, sir.

The smile and hope written on MAHUMPA's face drop away.

MAHUMPA

Then what are we supposed to do?

LARRY

He is a private person, so we couldn't find out as much as we would have liked. But we do know he is very fond of beautiful women.

MAHUMPA

Then let's send him a willing woman.

LARRY

It won't be that easy. Whoever he meets is run through a close background check, for his safety. Plus, people of Neugon are so loyal that they never betray their homeland.

MAHUMPA

Then what should we do?

MAHUMPA crumples up a piece of paper and tosses it to the ground. The conference room falls silent.

MAHUMPA

(slowly)

What about a woman who has lived there for a long time and has a very clean record?

MIKE

That could work, but who is she? Who would betray their homeland?

MAHUMPA

She is my daughter, who has been living in their city since her birth so she could get the best education in the world.

MIKE AND LARRY

It's worth a try.

MAHUMPA dismisses the meeting.

CUT TO:

INT. DANCE CLUB

MAHUMPA's daughter MEHER, who lives in Gracic, the city where RAUL, the son of KING DESOPATA, lives.

MEHER is enjoying a party with her friends in a club. She is beautiful and confident, and so charming that every man is staring at her.

MAN

(talking to his friends)

Check out that girl over there. Don't wait up for me.

He goes to MEHER with a glass of wine and a cigarette in his hand.

MAN

Hey, beautiful. Come with me and have some fun.

MEHER

Oh! Why not?

MEHER gets closer to the man. She puts both her hands on his chin and hits him with her right knee in between his legs.

MEHER

(laughing)

Was that fun? Did you enjoy it?

The MAN kneels to the ground, and all MEHER's friends start to laugh at him.

FADE TO:

Int. Beauty parlour – day

MEHER is enjoying a manicure. Her mobile starts to ring, and she sees that her father is calling. She takes the call, clearly excited and happy.

MEHER

Hi, Dad! What's up? Looks like you still remember me after such a long time.

MAHUMPA

Oh! My darling, I always remember about you, but I am so busy in my daily work that I don't get that much personal time. Anyway, what's going on there? How is my precious daughter?

MEHER

I am very good. I have so many friends that I get to see all the time. What about you, Dad?

MAHUMPA

I am also doing fine, but I'm stressed due to getting defeated by the Neugon army.

MEHER

But why, Dad? Why is this happening? What is keeping us from winning the war?

MAHUMPA

Because they are using advanced weapons. They have a very intelligent guy who makes very advanced weapons for the army.

MEHER

What are our scientists doing? Why haven't they invented anything better than he has?

MAHUMPA

Scientists like Einstein and Newton aren't born on regular basis. You never know when another one will come around.

MEHER

Then what should we do? How can we compete with that? Are we going to lose the war for good?

MAHUMPA

I didn't say that. Have you heard about how genes can be passed on to the next generation?

MEHER

What do you mean? What does that have to do with the war?

MAHUMPA

I know this is a lot to ask, but I want you to make RAUL, their genius scientist, attracted to you. If you can sleep with him, we can take his DNA and use it against him. But the important thing is that your child needs to be the most intelligent person in the world. Then we can finally defeat our enemies.

MEHER

But, Dad, doesn't that mean that the child could end up normal like me?

MAHUMPA

Leave it to me. I will take care of that. It would be easy to take the DNA and grow it in a lab, focusing on the genes that we want to cultivate. You wouldn't even need to give birth. All you need to do is come to me after you have had sex with him. Preferably within 12 hours of doing so. Do this for your own planet Domento, as a duty for our land.

MEHER

Okay. I trust you.

CUT TO:

INT. MEHER'S HOUSE

MIKE and LARRY arrive at MEHER's home.

MIKE

MEHER, look.

(Shows her a photo of RAUL)

RAUL is quite simple and is attracted to charming women. And he is very conscious about his health too. You can see him jogging in St. Stapula Park at 4:30 in the morning, but no one ever sees him leave.

LARRY

So 4:30 is the only time for you to impress him.

MEHER

Fine by me. Let's do it.

CUT TO:

EXT. PARK

RAUL is arriving at the park for jogging, with his four bodyguards around him. They approach the gate of the park. MEHER is at the gate, wearing a white shirt, white Bermuda shorts, and a white hairband. She and two friends are arguing with the GATEKEEPER.

MEHER

(Aggressively)

Let me in!

Gatekeeper

Sorry, ma'am, I can't let you come in. This is the time for sir RAUL's jog, and he will be here any minute.

MEHER

(Aggressively)

So what?

RAUL walks towards the park entrance. MEHER pretends like she has not seen him.

Gatekeeper

Oh! Hello, Mr. RAUL.

RAUL

(Annoyed)

What's going on here? What are you arguing about?

GATEKEEPER

This girl wants to go jogging at the same time as you do. I keep telling her that this is your private time at the park.

RAUL

(Angry)

Hey, this is my time. You can't be here. I need to be left alone.

MEHER

But I am not going to use the whole grounds. And I'm only in this area for a week. We want to jog here, not play football or be destructive.

RAUL

Just shut your mouth and leave.

MEHER closes her mouth and starts to silently cry.

RAUL gets a better look at her and seems to feel sorry for her.

RAUL

(Turning to gatekeeper)

Call the guard to check her out and give her a permit for a week. Then she can come at the park at the same time as I do.

MEHER

(happily)

Thank you, sir. Thank you so much.

RAUL moves through the open gate without saying anything to her.

FADE TO:

RAUL is doing his jogging on the track and notices MEHER tightening her shoelace.

Her hairs are going across her right cheek. This draws RAUL's attention. He moves toward MEHER.

But she passes by without talking to him.

After some time, RAUL sees that MEHER has fallen on the ground and that her friends are standing around her.

RAUL

(To his bodyguards)

What happened over there? Go check it out. I don't want anything dangerous in this park.

A BODYGUARD goes over to MEHER and examines her, then returns to RAUL.

BODYGUARD

The woman, MEHER, seems to have twisted her ankle.

RAUL

Okay, then get her to my house so she can have proper first aid.

BODYGUARD

Right away, sir.

The BODYGUARD goes back to MEHER.

BODYGUARD

Mr. RAUL has asked us to take you to his home for first aid.

MEHER

No, don't worry about it. I'm fine…

RAUL walks up to her.

RAUL

This is not anything special. It's no big deal. I would do this for everyone, so get in the car and let my experts give you first aid.

MEHER doesn't resist and stays quiet. The plan is working, but it seems dangerous to go to his home so quickly. Her hands shake in her lap as she waits anxiously for the car to stop.

FADE TO:

int. RAUL's house

A doctor offers some medicine to MEHER, but she won't take it.

RAUL

Don't worry. It won't hurt you.

MEHER

No.

RAUL

Trust me. It will not hurt you. It's okay.

MEHER

I trust only those who are close to me.

RAUL

Then I am talking to you as a friend.

MEHER

How can we be friends? We only met for the first time today.

RAUL

Then we can meet again this evening for dinner.

MEHER

Done.

The doctor gives her a pain pill and wraps up her ankle.

MEHER goes to her hotel.

CUT TO:

RAUL picks up MEHER at her hotel. They go to an upscale restaurant and get a private table for two.

An accommodating server greets them.

RAUL

They specialize in continental food. Only the best, of course. What would you like to have, MEHER?

MEHER

(Flirtatiously)

Okay, so you know a lot about this restaurant, but you don't know much about me.

RAUL

(Intrigued)

And what does that mean?

MEHER

If I go out with someone on a date, I order whatever they pick out for me.

RAUL

(to server)

Then please bring one plate of my favorite dish.

MEHER

Why only one order? Why not eat with me?

RAUL

Well, my way to do a date is to first get the food of my choice and then my date's choice as the second course.

MEHER

I like your style.

RAUL

By the way, what brings you to this city?

MEHER

I am here to visit some friends and go sightseeing.

RAUL

Oh, so where have you gone so far?

MEHER

I got in town late last night, and I spent my morning with you. Now I'm spending my evening with you, so I haven't had time to go exploring at all.

RAUL

Then you should come with me tomorrow. I can show you everything of interest here.

FADE OUT.

Ext. Restaurant

RAUL

You know, it's rather late now. Why don't you stay at my guesthouse?

MEHER

Why not? It will be nice to have company in this strange city.

MEHER takes her luggage to RAUL's guesthouse.

CUT TO:

Int. guest house - morning

MEHER is asleep. The doorbell rings, and MEHER gets up and opens the door.

PERSON

Good morning, ma'am.

MEHER

Morning.

PERSON

Mr. RAUL is waiting for you at the breakfast table.

MEHER

Okay, I will be there in 10 minutes.

PERSON

Okay, ma'am. I'll let him know.

MEHER gets ready very quickly and heads to the breakfast table.

MEHER

Good morning to all of you.

EVERYONE

Good morning

King Desopata

Did you sleep well, MEHER?

MEHER

Oh, yes! It was really nice.

FADE OUT.

Int. The hall Outside the dining room

RAUL

How much time do you need to get ready?

MEHER

Just an hour.

                    RAUL

                (Flirtatiously)

See you then.

                                              CUT TO:

EXT. GRACIC

RAUL takes MEHER to a museum and to the historical
monuments of the city.

Int. Club - night

                   MANAGER

Good evening. Welcome to our club. Please have a seat
wherever you like.

                    RAUL

Thank you. What's going on here today?

                   MANAGER

The club is hosting a competition for teams of two, where one
partner picks a song, and the other partner must dance to it.

                    MEHER

Wow! That sounds fun. Why don't we participate in it?

                   MANAGER

Great, thank you. Names?

MEHER

I'm MEHER, and this is RAUL.

The MANAGER starts to fill out a form.

RAUL

No, I am not going to do that.

MEHER

Why not? Please? It will be so much fun.

RAUL

Nope, no way.

MEHER

Please, please, please?

RAUL

Are you going to keep asking until I agree to it?

MEHER

I sure am. Please, please, please can we do it?

RAUL

Fine, fine. We'll do it.

MANAGER

Thanks for your interest. I'll call you up shortly.

The MANAGER heads to the front and announces their names.

RAUL picks violin music, and MEHER picks [music type] music. Both of them do well. The closer they dance to each other, the more RAUL is attracted to MEHER.

When the contest finishes, they get announced as the winners. Their prize was that they got free food and drinks for the rest of the night.

They order drink after drink and eventually end up kissing each other.

To fulfill her task of having sex with RAUL, MEHER presses up against him and convinces RAUL to go back to his place.

INT. Raul's guest house - night

By the time they arrive, they have sobered up, and it gets heated quickly.

They have passionate sex and fall asleep in each other's arms.

FADE TO:

Int. Raul's GUEST HOUSE - Morning

RAUL is waking up, still undressed from the night before. MEHER is nowhere to be seen, nor is her luggage.

RAUL

MEHER, where are you?

RAUL searches for her, but she's left no trace of her visit. RAUL eventually finds a note from her on the door.

MEHER (V.O.)

Hi, RAUL, this is MEHER. This is embarrassing to admit, but I feel so guilty for having sex before marriage. I promised myself long ago that I would wait, but I couldn't help myself when I met you. Now I feel so guilty, and I can't bear to face you. I hate to leave without saying goodbye, but it would only make it harder for me to go. I enjoyed our time together, and I'll never forget it. Thank you for all your kindness and company. Please forgive me. I'm so sorry.

RAUL is clearly upset, but he gets dressed and leaves, tossing MEHER's note into the trash.

CUT TO:

Ext. boat dock - morning

MEHER, wearing a disguise, gets on a series of boats to go to the secret meeting place. It is late at night when she gets off the last boat.

CUT TO:

Int. Laboratory

MEHER runs into the lab and hugs her father.

MEHER

Did I make it in time? Is it still worth it?

MAHUMPA

Yes. Good job, sweetheart.

The lab assistants head over.

MAHUMPA

Please don't let my daughter's hard work go to waste. Our homeland is counting on it.

CUT TO:

Doctors hold up a test tube and begin to do experiments with it. Different chemical reactions occur. They discuss genetics as they combine RAUL's sperm and MEHER's egg, and then set it up to grow.

FADE IN:

Two months have passed. MEHER is finally allowed to see her son for the first time.

MEHER

He's beautiful!

MAHUMPA

I agree. Good job, MEHER.

DR. STEPHENS

What name would you like to give him?

MEHER

I'd like to name him after both my father and the baby's father. How about. RAHUMPA?

MAHUMPA

Wow, I am honored. Thank you, MEHER.

CUT TO:

Ext. Laboratory – afternoon

Doctors and scientists do tests, and RAHUMPA is already showing signs of great intelligence and curiosity.

A year has passed. RAHUMPA has grown to the size of an eight-year-old.

MEHER is living down the hallway from the lab and visits with her son every day.

DR. STEPHENS greets MAHUMPA.

MAHUMPA

Hi, how is everything? How is the baby? Is he doing well? Is he meeting our expectations?

DR. STEPHENS

Please come and have a look at him.

There, he sees how quickly RAHUMPA has grown. MEHER is clearly proud of him. The doctors show MAHUMPA all the brain scans and medical readings. RAHUMPA is in perfect health.

MAHUMPA is overjoyed.

MAHUMPA

When can we take him home?

DR. STEPHENS

We're doing our final inspections. He should be ready in two days.

MAHUMPA

Okay, see you soon. Thanks again, DR. STEPHENS. Please let me know if you need anything.

DR. STEPHENS

Okay, sir.

MEHER

Of course, Dad.

FADE TO:

Ext. Laboratory

MAHUMPA arrives. He and MEHER are very excited.

RAHUMPA is still in a glass container, connected to tubes for nourishment and medical readings. He is still asleep. The doctors do a countdown from 10.

The doctors begin to remove the tubes and disconnect him from the machines.

After a few minutes, the boy starts to cry, but then, he stops and looks around, examining each face in the room.

DR. STEPHENS

Hi, little boy, how are you?

MEHER

Say "I am good."

RAHUMPA looks unsure of himself and finally speaks in a wavering tone.

RAHUMPA

Hi, little boy, how are you? Say I am good.

Everyone cheers and hugs.

MAHUMPA

Thank you; you did a good job!

MEHER

Thanks, Dad.

DR. STEPHENS

You're welcome.

MAHUMPA

Are you ready to take him home for a little while, MEHER?

MEHER

That would be wonderful.

DR. STEPHENS

(handing MEHER a checklist)

You need to do these tests and ensure that he is adjusting well. Any time he does something or something changes; you need to write it down. We're also going to send an INTERN to help you out.

CUT TO:

Int. Mahumpa's home

MAHUMPA and MEHER both come to MAHUMPA'S home and are very happy and excited.

They take RAHUMPA to a room full of toys. As with other children, he is excited to see the toys but seems unsure as to which he can play with. MEHER tells RAHMUPA that those are all his toys and shows him what to do.

Two days later, he is bored with the toys, even those designed for eight-year-old children. The INTERN has several pages of notes already.

MAHUMPA calls the INTERN over.

MAHUMPA

Can you please go to a toy store and buy puzzle toys and games, as well as toys that talk while doing things?

A short time later, the INTERN comes back to the house with baskets full of toys.

RAHUMPA is excited to try the new toys and games. By the end of the evening, he has completed all his puzzles and can make some of the sounds that his toys make.

MAHUMPA surprises RAHUMPA with a personal tablet that he can use to learn new things.

FADE TO:

INT. LaboratorY

Five days later, MAHUMPA and MEHER return to the lab.

RECEPTIONIST

Good morning. Good to see you again.

MAHUMPA

Good morning. We're here to see DR. STEPHENS.

RECEPTIONIST

Let me get in touch with him.

The RECEPTIONIST presses a button.

RAHUMPA

Good morning, sister.

RECEPTIONIST

(smiling)

Good morning, little boy.

DR. STEPHENS arrives.

DR. STEPHENS

Good morning, everyone.

RAHUMPA

Good morning, Doctor.

DR. STEPHENS

(Impressed)

Wow! Sounds like you're starting to talk on your own. Now I need to do some checks. We'll also get you vaccinated today. All the normal things for a child.

MAHUMPA and MEHER wait outside. After some time has passed, DR. STEPHENS comes out of the lab with RAHUMPA.

DR. STEPHENS

Everything looks good so far. Please try to get him a special tutor. He's about ready to enter school. I'm sure you're nervous, but he will be someone very special.

MEHER appoints many teachers for RAHUMPA. In five years, RAHUMPA is able to graduate high school.

He becomes a scientist and is now ready to serve the Domento Army.

Right before RAHUMPA starts his duty, MAHUMPA takes him to a war museum, showing him what the Neugon army has done. He gives him some personal photos from the war, mostly of RAUL's machines and weapons.

Then, he takes him to an office building, showing him a room filled with objects covered by sheets.

MAHUMPA

Grandson, I have something special here for you.

MAHUMPA removes the sheets, revealing military equipment.

RAHUMPA

What is this, Granddad?

MAHUMPA

Our soldiers acquired these weapons, but we have yet to understand how to use them. With your intelligence, I'm sure you'll figure out what to do. I hope you can even make them better than before.

RAHUMPA

I will try my best, Granddad.

The next room over has a nice desk and several comfortable seats.

MAHUMPA

This is your office now.

MEHER

We are so proud of you, son.

RAHUMPA

(Happily)

Thank you! Thank you so much.

RAHUMPA works with the technology and develops weapons like the one from the first scene. This one can expel fire much further. He designs a gun that can shoot lightning bolts, even in the vacuum of space.

He also develops the fastest planes of the time and sets up a lab on a remote planet that is difficult to survive on without advanced technology.

Eventually, he returns to society.

Ten years later, he settles down with a family and has two sons of his own. With a sense of secrecy and privacy like his father RAUL, he moves back to the remote planet with his family.

He makes a living by designing custom weapons, kidnapping royals, and holding them for ransom. As his business develops, he sends people to destroy the labs of other competing scientists, preventing them from making better tech.

CUT TO:

Ext. military complex – day

RAUL's territory is very quiet.

Camera goes over the ranking officers of the army.

The officers look tense.

Camera pans to show a projected message from RAHUMPA.

RAHUMPA

(Threatening)

Give me your royal family members, or prepare for war.

FADE TO:

Int. RAUL's room – evening

RAUL is sitting on his bed and looking at the clock. He looks upset and concerned.

RAUL

My territory has come into the great danger because our labs keep getting destroyed. How can my weapons get developed if we have no labs? RAHUMPA is dominating us with his technology. Our boundaries are getting smaller every day. What can we do to recover our former status?

RAUL seems to have an idea. He starts getting dressed and packing a bag. His WIFE comes into the room.

WIFE

(warmly)

What happened? Where are you going?

RAUL

(evasive)

Nothing! Nowhere. I'll be back soon.

RAUL leaves the room and orders someone to call all the great people all around the universe, all the great scientists of every place who are not happy with RAHUMPA. He sets up a special location and a way to telecast in with a special code if someone couldn't come in person.

CUT TO:

Int. RAUL's territory – afternoon

In a secret underground room, accessible only through access cards, a large group of scientists sit at a conference table. The hall is pristine and white, with heavy security at every door.

RAUL is greeting everyone who comes in.

RAUL

(friendly)

Good morning, everybody. We have gathered here to discuss the matter of dealing with RAHUMPA's disturbance across the universe. He doesn't want to listen to anyone trying to reason with him. He's like an escaped bull who will attack anyone who comes near him.

SCIENTIST #1

What are we supposed to do? He is using superior technology. We are not that strong, and neither are our weapons.

RAUL

(Aggressive)

Don't say that. If we unite, we can make a difference.

SCIENTIST #2

What do you mean? It's hopeless.

RAUL

(Assertively)

If we come together as a group and start a war against him, then we can do something. Do you understand me now?

SCIENTIST #3

(doubtful)

I am starting to understand, but can you please explain your plan in more detail?

RAUL

It's not a huge plan. We need to work together and prepare for war as we normally would. But this time, my son, ANTAL, will visit your labs with our army so that you can work without fear.

After the meeting finishes, everyone looks happy and heads home in a variety of spaceships. One person in particular heads back to RAHUMPA, notes in hand.

FADE TO:

Int. reception desk - moments later

The phone rings, and the RECEPTIONIST immediately answers. A 3-D image of a MYSTERIOUS PERSON appears in front of the touch-screen computer on the table. The MYSTERIOUS PERSON is wearing a cloak that obscures their identity.

MYSTERIOUS PERSON

I want to talk to RAHUMPA.

RECEPTIONIST

Who am I speaking to?

MYSTERIOUS PERSON

This is RONITTO.

RECEPTIONIST

Let me check.

The RECEPTIONIST mutes the call and contacts RAHUMPA.

RECEPTIONIST

Commander in Chief RAHUMPA, Mr. RONITTO wants to speak you on a call.

RAHUMPA

Okay, send the call to me.

RECEPTIONIST

Okay, sir.

(to RONITTO)

Okay, sir, you can talk to him. One moment, please.

RAHUMPA answers the call. He sets up the call so that they can see each other.

RAHUMPA

RONITTO, what is the news?

RONITTO (mysterious person)

The news is not good. That's why I am calling you.

RAHUMPA

Okay, then come in so we can discuss it.

The RECEPTIONIST unlocks the gate and allows RONITTO to enter the building.

RECEPTIONIST

Go down this hallway and take a right three times. The commander-in-chief will be on the right-hand side.

RONITTO passes by several laboratories as he walks down the hall. He peers in through a small window on the door. RAHUMPA is talking to two people. He is shouting at one of them.

RONITTO knocks and opens the door, and the room falls silent. The person who got shouted at starts drinking water.

RAHUMPA

Welcome. Sit anywhere you like.

RONITTO enters the room, sits on the chair closest to RAHUMPA, and says nothing.

After a few minutes, RAHUMPA asks him if he wants water, but RONITTO is still silent.

RAHUMPA

What happened, RONITTO? Weren't you going to tell me something very important?

RONITTO

Yes, but I wanted to have some privacy. I thought your advisers would have left by now.

RAHUMPA

Not to worry. This is my son, following in my footsteps, and my grandfather, MAHUMPA, the former president of this territory. Please feel free to discuss what you've learned.

RONITTO

Oh! Yes. Thank you.

(tensely)

RAUL is creating an army by turning the whole universe against you. They're joining together to fight you.

MAHUMPA

What is his strategy? What did they discuss?

RONITTO

He didn't say much. But he wants to unite everyone against you, even the ones who have surrendered to you before. He is preparing them for war. He's even going to send his son to their laboratories so they can work on new technology without fear.

MAHUMPA seems concerned, but RAHUMPA is confidant and taking it lightly.

RAHUMPA

His son is only 24 years old. The first fight with any of my soldiers, he's a goner.

RAHUMPA pours some drink in his glass and holds it up as a toast.

Cut to:

Int. RAUL's office - Day

RAUL takes his son, ANTAL, into the military hallway to look at the gallery of their ancestors.

RAUL

We come from a very brave, very proud family. And we know very well that war cannot be won with good weapons alone. There are several key aspects: timing, strategy, mindset, powerful weapons, and, most importantly, bravery.

RAUL takes ANTAL to a laboratory. RAUL unlocks the door with a voice password, hand print, and retina scan.

The room is full of weapons in glass cases. RAUL removes a red wooden weapon. It has a broad nose with a wide barrel. RAUL goes into another case and grabs a green weapon with an adjustable mouth.

RAUL

This red one in my left hand is for creating a stream of fire. But it's better than a standard flamethrower. The green one in my right hand is in case something of ours gets set on fire.

ANTAL

Thank you, Dad.

RAUL

Now I am going to show you how to use these and some other weapons.

He opens his computer and drags a 3-D representation of the missile launching station from the screen to display on the ground.

RAUL

So then you take the graph from over here and line it up with this other graph in front of the missile. Then, simply tap on it.

The computer generates a path and showed the speed and time for how long it would take to hit the target. RAUL launches a 3-D image of a missile.

ANTAL

Wow! It's amazing!

RAUL

No, it's not. There are many amazing things at the real war front. This was a defensive move. Try an offensive one.

RAUL drags another graph and some vehicles off the screen.

RAUL

You can see that small, pilot-less helicopter. Try flying it.

ANTAL flies it as high as he can go. RAUL pulls the graph closer, and then taps on it. A missile launches and hits the helicopter.

RAUL shows him a series of more weapons. RAUL sends someone to get him one of each.

Not much later, someone arrives with a large cart full of the requested weapons.

RAUL

Okay, son, you are almost prepared for your journey. Now, everything will depend on your decisions at war.

ANTAL

Exactly, but how will I carry all of this?

RAUL

Actually, that is a good question. Let's go to the next lab.

In another lab, they're many other scientists working at the same time. This lab is much smaller than the previous one.

RAUL

Excuse me, but my son and I need to work. For the good of our homeland.

The scientists look unhappy but clear out.

RAUL

Son, this is the most important lab of mine. Anyone can make weapons. But keeping them safe and comfortably with you is quite difficult.

ANTAL

That makes sense.

RAUL opens a compartment and a pair of glasses comes out of it. ANTAL puts the glasses on.

RAUL

These are my best glasses. You can wear them any time. If anything important or dangerous happens, click this button at the edge of the frame.

RAUL presses the button. The lenses take on a green hue.

RAUL

No matter where you are, you can use night vision or day vision.

RAUL clicks the button on the other side of the glasses. The graphs from earlier pop up on the corner of the lens.

RAUL

You can see all the graphs for missiles. If you say "parabola," it will show you the parabolic path and nature of the missile. These glasses are very advanced, as they can take your audio orders and always aim missiles accurately.

RAUL opens a new drawer, and a wallet comes out of it.

RAUL

This wallet is unique and the most important thing I can give you. You wanted to know how you were going to keep track of all those weapons. This is the tool for that. The spray on the desk is capable of shrinking anything and everything--besides people and animals, of course. We're going to shrink your weapons, and you'll be able to access them by pressing these letter combinations on the inside of the wallet. The weapon will then come out.

ANTAL

Wow! How will they come back to their original form?

RAUL

For that, before going out, you need to have this powder on your hands. When you touch any shrunk object with the powder, it will return to its original size. It is waterproof, so you don't have to worry about sweating it off.

(beat)

Now you have your weapons and your missile monitor. Guard these with your life. And if you need any help, let me know right away.

ANTAL

Thank you, Father.

RAUL looks at a photo of his employees.

RAUL

I met your friend Dante. I think he should go with you.

ANTAL

What? Why?

RAUL

I think it will help motivate others to fight against RAHUMPA.

ANTAL

Okay, my dear father.

Now ANTAL has gone for his first journey to meet a scientist named SIR GEORGE WILLINGTON, heading to the territory of Saint Thomas.

SIR WILLINGTON seems to be a very intelligent person, but their labs are in very poor condition. The buildings are partially broken and have no gates.

ANTAL

What happened to here? Your lab should be nice-looking. There should be a gate so that no one can come inside without permission.

WILLINGTON

(sad)

Yes, you are right, but the matter of fact is that we need sufficient resources inside the building that we have. RAHUMPA's troops have been breaking our stuff, because they don't want any kind of gate in the front of lab so that they can enter the lab anytime. I feel much better now that you are here to protect me.

ANTAL

Thanks, sir, for having this much belief in me.

After a little time, SIR GEORGE WILLINGTON's team members enter the lab.

There is sun in the sky, winds are blowing, and then clouds move. Night time comes.

Int. RAHUMPA's office

RAHUMPA calls his crew to the Saint Thomas territory.

RAHUMPA

RAUL's son, ANTAL, is in your territory at the Willington lab, I want you to go that place and make ANTAL leave.

CREW MEMBER

Okay, sir, as you say. He will not be there tomorrow morning.

Ext. Willington lab - nighttime

It is very quiet.

ANTAL

DANTE, something should be happening.

DANTE

Oh! Yes, but maybe they got scared because they know I am here with you.

They both laugh.

DANTE

You should wear your glasses to look for suspicious activity.

After a little while, some kind of noise comes out of the bushes.

ANTAL can see something green inside the bushes due to his night vision glasses.

ANTAL uses his wallet to take out a shotgun. He fires it at the bushes. There is another loud noise. When they look at the target, they find that it was a goat.

ANTAL

Oh! Shit, I am sorry, I thought it was the enemy.

DANTE

It's okay! It happens sometimes.

Another noise comes from bushes. DANTE pulls out his gun.

ANTAL

Don't shoot. It might be another animal.

Three people step out from the bushes, with menacing expressions. Two of them go toward the lab entrance, SHOOTER #3 climbing onto the roof, and SHOOTER #1 laughs and points his gun at ANTAL.

SHOOTER #1

Go home! Do you want to get killed?

DANTE immediately shoots and kills SHOOTER #1.

SHOOTER #2 points a flamethrower at DANTE.

ANTAL grabs his water-thrower and tries to use it on DANTE. But it can't shoot far enough.

SHOOTER #3 jumps from the roof, but DANTE immediately shoots him and kills him.

SHOOTER #2 uses a flying machine to create smoke for cover.

ANTAL uses his glasses, takes his rocket gun out, and fires it at SHOOTER #2.

SHOOTER #2 runs but gets hit, the explosion also hitting his ship.

RAHUMPA is watching this in the form of 3-D images like his father once did and asks who is with DANTE. But no one answers.

CUT TO:

Int. Laboratory - moments later

All the scientists, along with SIR WILLINGTON, come out of the lab and see the dead bodies RAHUMPA's shooters.

WILLINGTON

Thank you for saving us. But be careful. They'll come back with more power.

ANTAL

It's okay. We are here so that no one will be able to disturb you.

FADE IN:

Ext. Laboratory - morning

Many people come to find out what happened that night. The PRESIDENT arrives in a long, black vehicle with security guards. They approach ANTAL and congratulate him.

PRESIDENT

You have done a very good job; this is what we need from you.

(taking a breath)

But be careful. They will come back to get revenge.

ANTAL

Don't worry, sir. We are ready.

PRESIDENT

Once all of this is over, I'll treat you to a nice meal at my house.

ANTAL

As long as people don't need us to protect them!

CUT TO:

Int. Tent - night

There is the sound of a flying machine moving very quickly. Then, the sound of gunshots. DANTE wakes up ANTAL.

ANTAL

What happened?

DANTE answers with a shrug. He runs to where the sound came from and hides behind a tree. ANTAL hides behind a large stone.

At the site, there is a woman who is doing some kind of practice work of firing firearms.

DANTE and ANTAL approach the guard.

DANTE

What's going on here?

GUARD

She is a princess of this territory, and she is very fond of training with firearms. I don't recommend getting too close.

ANTAL

Let's head back then. Thanks for the information.

FADE TO:

Int. Tent

DANTE

I think we should talk to SIR WILLINGTON. It would be nice if we could go to the president's house for lunch.

ANTAL

What will we say to him? That we were too busy this morning but that we are free now? Ooh, I have an idea. What if we tell him that we wanted to talk to SIR WILLINGTON about nuclear war?

DANTE

No... that's not a good idea. Let's go talk to him directly.

They get dressed and get on the plane, then fly to the president's home. They are greeted by a GATEKEEPER.

GATEKEEPER

Do you have an appointment with the PRESIDENT?

ANTAL

No, but tell him that ANTAL is here to meet him.

The GATEKEEPER dials the PRESIDENT's office.

GATEKEEPER

Hello, sir, ANTAL and his friend want to meet you.

PRESIDENT

Okay, let them come in.

The GATEKEEPER sends them ahead. The palace is huge. ANTAL sees the PRESIDENT'S DAUGHTER from earlier, and they make eye contact.

The PRESIDENT approaches ANTAL and DANTE.

DANTE

Hello, Mr. President, how are you?

ANTAL

Hello, sir, how are you doing today?

PRESIDENT

I am very good. How about you? I'm surprised you're here so soon.

ANTAL

Oh, we thought it might be nice to take a break and visit with you. Sorry for the inconvenience.

The PRESIDENT'S DAUGHTER enters the room. She and ANTAL stare at each other. The PRESIDENT notices.

PRESIDENT

Oh! She is my daughter ANGELICA.

(to ANGELICA)

What are you doing here?

ANGELICA (pRESIDENT'S DAUGHTER)

I came to see who these people are. They don't look like they're from around here.

PRESIDENT

They are from KING DESOPATA's territory. They're going to protect our scientists as they work. This is ANTAL, and this is DANTE.

ANGELICA

Good. ANTAL, when you are free, you should teach me about war strategies.

ANTAL

Come by tomorrow. SIR WILLINGTON is taking the day off.

ANTAL and DANTE eat dinner with the PRESIDENT and his family.

FADE TO:

Int. Meeting hall - evening

RAHUMPA is holding a meeting, and his information techs provide him with data from their satellites.

FADE OUT.

Ext. Willington lab - evening

SIR WILLINGTON and two of his team members greet ANTAL.

SIR WILLINGTON

I have something amazing for you now that we have the PRESIDENT's full support. I've worked on it for the past 6 years. It works as a special transporter. You don't have to carry your weapons by hand--it will carry them for you.

ANTAL

Wow! How does it work?

WILLINGTON

You send an address via e-mail to the supercomputer of that address, so whichever lab you store your belongings in. Once your supervisor accepts the storage request, it links itself to their inventory.

All you need to do is put down the address of the place you want to connect and it will directly send the e-mail to the supercomputer of that address and if the supervisor accepts that then it link itself to the inventory of that place

The next day, ANTAL contacts his father, RAUL.

ANTAL

Hi, Dad. I hope you're doing well. SIR WILLINGTON has a new transportation system that I wanted to talk to you about. It allows us to remotely access our equipment so we don't have to carry it everywhere.

RAUL

Wow, that sounds fantastic.

ANTAL

All I have to do is send a request to you, and then I can use all of our equipment.

RAUL

Okay, son

ANTAL tests the equipment and is impressed. He spends the rest of the night preparing for the visit from ANGELICA.

CUT TO:

Int. RAHUMPA's office

RAHUMPA

I'm very displeased about losing to that boy.
His followers and team leaders say nothing.

RAHUMPA

Someone, go keep an eye on ANTAL. Tell me everything he does. Leave nothing out.

TEAM LEADER

Why is it so important? He's one person.

RAHUMPA

RAUL and his family are powerful. More than you realize. I don't care which of you does it, but someone here needs to go and spy on ANTAL. Don't get caught.

FADE OUT.

Int. RAHUMPA's office

RAHUMPA's TEAM LEADER arrives with videos and documentation of ANTAL spending time with ANGELICA.

RAHUMPA

Who is that girl? She is beautiful.

TEAM LEADER

We're not sure.

RAHUMPA

Is that his girlfriend? Find out. Tell me everything they do. Two days pass.

RAHUMPA

What's new?

TEAM LEADER

She seems to be in a romantic relationship with ANTAL.

RAHUMPA

The prepare for the next attack. And this time, I don't want to lose anyone, so be cautious. Let him see you nearby. Let him pursue you. While you do that, I will kidnap the girlfriend. I want to marry her,.

RAHUMPA enters the territory, with five people staying close to him. They stop and fire at the lab, but it seems as though no one is there. RAHUMPA splits off from the group.

ANTAL and DANTE come out and see RAHUMPA's people. Three of them run, while two start randomly firing their guns.

DANTE

Chase after them! I'll deal with the shooters.

RAHUMPA checks inside the building. Using a voice-changing device to call for ANGELICA, he makes himself sound like ANTAL. His plane deploys a net as soon as RAHUMPA lures ANGELICA out of the building. They pull her into the ship and head for their home planet. Angelica fights back, but she was not able to get out hand of Rahumpa.

RAHUMPA sends a special signal to the crew to say that the mission was accomplished. They hop into their nearby jets and fly away as quickly as they can.

DANTE and ANTAL are confused, so they communicate with their walkie-talkies.

ANTAL

Did you catch anyone?

DANTE

No, they flew away. You?

ANTAL

Same here.

DANTE

That's strange. Was it a distraction?

ANTAL

Let's go home and check on everyone.

They arrive at their home near the laboratory.

ANTAL

ANGELICA, now you can come out.

But there is no response. And then both of them try to find her everywhere in the camp, but she is not there. ANTAL gets sad, but DANTE tries to track her on the radar. Unfortunately, he is unable to find her.

Both of them are very sad and have nothing to do for now.

CUT TO:

RAHUMPA is flying ANGELICA to his territory.

On the surface below, a girl and a boy are fighting. The boy, BASHIN, sees the aircraft and points it out to his father, the KING. The KING does some scans and sees that it is a case of kidnapping. He connects to their radio.

KING

There's a woman struggling on your ship. Let her free, or I will kill you.

RAHUMPA

Just try it.

The KING and his soldiers increase their speed and get closer to RAHUMPA's ship. The soldiers begin firing. RAHUMPA releases a missile that destroys the soldiers' ships.

The KING gets angry and speeds up, then releases a missile at RAHUMPA's plane. RAHUMPA's plane shakes, and he releases a missile at the king's ship. Nothing happens because his plane is missile-proof.

The KING taps into RAHUMPA's radio again.

KING

(Laughing)

Are you still going to stick around? Or are we done yet?

RAHUMPA

Just wait and see.

He shoots at the KING's plane with an electric current. The plane shakes. The KING fires back at him, but RAHUMPA evades the shot.

FADE IN:

The KING's son, BASHIN, is watching from the planet below. He's smiling and cheering his father on.

BASHIN

Dad!

FADE OUT.:

KING

(Angry)

Just release the woman!

RAHUMPA

(very angry)

Computer, what is wrong with my weapons? Why are my weapons are not working on him?

COMPUTER

He is using an electromagnetic shield.

RAHUMPA

Okay, then make a net of laser beams with electromagnetic currents and fire it at him.

The missile fires. The net of laser beams glimmers with a red electromagnetic current, with light blue sparkling around it.

When it gets closer to the plane, the KING's plane's shield comes out, but the electromagnetic current neutralizes it so it is a net of laser beams. The net pierces through the ship, cutting the ship and the KING's body in pieces, which float in space.

FADE IN:

Ext. KING's planet

The KING's SON, BASIN, who was watching all this, gets sad and cries a single tear, but he wipes it away with his sleeve.

BASIN

Dad, you did a good job, but I will get revenge for your death.

FADE OUT.

Int. RAHUMPA's plane

ANGELICA feels hopeless while RAHUMPA celebrates. She tried to escape, but it was not easy.

RAHUMPA

Quit moping. I'm having a good time. I am in love with you. You are so beautiful, I want to marry you.

ANGELICA goes to a corner and tries to ignore RAHUMPA.

ANGELICA

If I had my guns, this would be a different story.

Ext. RAHUMPA's territory

Everything is advanced, clean, and systemized. RAHUMPA is greeted by a GUARD.

GUARD

Congratulations to you, Sir. Everyone is safe, and you have ANTAL's loved one. Mission accomplished.

RAHUMPA

No, not accomplished. It's the beginning. Take ANGELICA to the barricades. I'll deal with her later. Do something, I want her to be my wife.

CUT TO

Int - ANTAL's camp - day

ANTAL is worried about ANGELICA. He calls his father to discuss the issue.

ANTAL

You know, Dad, I have not explained this whole situation to the PRESIDENT. I am not able to face him after this happened.

RAUL

It's okay, my son. You are brave, and they wanted to distract you. Do you want me to talk to the PRESIDENT for you?

ANTAL

No, Dad, I will talk to him myself. I must write my own story. I'm going to try to relax for a while. Now that I've talked to you, I feel a lot better.

RAUL

Well done, my boy. Never feel alone. Each generation must make its own path and follow those who are willing to guide them.

ANTAL leaves and informs the PRESIDENT of where ANGELICA has gone.

RAHUMPA is leaving the prison where ANGELICA is being held. He goes to check surveillance, only to find that his PEOPLE are watching it carefully, examining the research being done across the universe.

When RAHUMPA enters, all of them stand up.

RAHUMPA

(Angry)

What's going on? Aren't you supposed to be doing research or something?

All the PEOPLE are silent. No one has anything to say to him.

RAHUMPA

I'm glad you've been working so hard lately, but we need to get back to it. We have a project that needs our complete attention. Focus on moving the satellites toward ANTAL's region. Let me know if he makes any moves.

All the PEOPLE

Yes, sir.

The move their focus towards ANTAL, who is sitting with ANGELICA's father, the PRESIDENT of that territory.

RAHUMPA

Keep me updated. Leave nothing out.

All the PEOPLE

Yes, sir.

FADE TO:

Int. President's dining room

PRESIDENT

(Angry)

I thought you would protect us, but you couldn't even keep my daughter from getting kidnapped. How can I believe that you'll protect my people?

ANTAL

Sir, I am so sorry. Believe me: I will bring your daughter back. I'd like to work together to find out exactly where ANGELICA is. Then, I'll head back to my father's land and use his technology to find and rescue her. I don't want to waste a single moment.

PRESIDENT

Let's go and check it on the satellite.

They head to the control room to watch the surveillance tapes. There are two PEOPLE watching the radar for the whole city.

PRESIDENT

What's going on? Did you see anything last night?

The PEOPLE stand up.

PERSON #1

No, sir. We didn't see anything.

ANTAL

How is that possible?

PERSON #2

No, our radar screen was clear all the night

ANTAL

How is that possible? Weren't there cameras?

ANTAL grows silent and begins to think.

ANTAL

Maybe his plane cannot be caught on the radar, but our satellites should have videos.

ANTAL and PRESIDENT go to the satellites' surveillance center. The PEOPLE stand up and greet them.

PRESIDENT

Did you see anything last night?

SECTION HEAD

Well, we did see some unusual activity. What are you asking about in particular?

PRESIDENT

I'd like to see the video from last night, about 10 to 11 p.m. My daughter ANGELICA vanished around them.

SECTION HEAD

Yes, sir, we have some satellite cameras that are designed to track everything.

PRESIDENT

Then I would like to see the videos for the Willington lab for last night.

They check every video but find nothing.

PRESIDENT

Guards, seize him. He is a liar.

The guards approach ANTAL and grasp his wrists.

SECTION HEAD

Wait, wait! There was supposed to be no wind last night, but there's movement in these trees.

Everyone gathers around the screen. There are strong winds, blue and red lights, and a few types of planes. The video shows everything that happened.

The guards are about to take ANTAL out of the room in shackles.

PRESIDENT

Release him! I am very sorry for not believing you. I love ANGELICA, and I am so worried about her.

ANTAL

I'm worried too, sir. I love her, and I want to be with her for the rest of my life.

DANTE

Okay, I'm glad we got that cleared up. But let's figure out how to get her back from RAHUMPA.

CUT TO:

Int. meeting hall - morning

PRESIDENT and his 10 military heads are sitting in a room.

Camera shot sweeps over the heads.

PRESIDENT

(Sadly)

As you all know, RAHUMPA kidnapped my daughter, ANGELICA. I don't know what to do. Please give me your advice.

All the PEOPLE were silent for a short while.

PERSON #1

We should go for war.

PERSON #2

I agree!

PRESIDENT

Do we want to fight RAHUMPA this way? You know how much power he wields.

And the camera is moving to every person, but there is a PERSON #3 who is quiet during the whole meeting. This PERSON #3 listens to everyone's suggestions. After a short while, PERSON #4 speaks up.

PERSON #4

We could apologize to RAHUMPA for helping RAUL and promise that we won't do it again.

KING

(shouting)

Oh! Wonderful idea! You are very wise. Will we still be able to live with honor after we enact your plan?

It is silent again.

PERSON #3

Why did RAHUMPA kidnap your daughter?

PRESIDENT

I don't know. Maybe it's because we are helping RAUL with his idea for defeating RAHUMPA.

PERSON #3

Where was she when RAHUMPA kidnapped her?

PRESIDENT

She was with ANTAL.

PERSON #3

Then why are we worrying about all this? Ask ANTAL what he is going to do about getting ANGELICA back. It's not RAUL's fault here. It's ANTAL's fault too. If not for him, ANGELICA wouldn't be in this situation.

The PRESIDENT considers his words carefully.

PRESIDENT

I'll see what I can do. This meeting is dissolved. Say nothing of this to anyone outside this room.

ALL THE PEOPLE

Yes, sir.

CUT TO

Int. Personal office - evening

ANTAL came to meet the PRESIDENT with DANTE and knocked on the door before coming in. The PRESIDENT is sitting in the office and reading a file.

ANTAL

Good evening, sir.

PRESIDENT

Good evening. Can I help you?

ANTAL

Just trying to find a way to ANGELICA free from RAHUMPA.

PRESIDENT

Please keep thinking about it. Have you come up with anything?

ANTAL

Yes, but have you had any ideas as well?

PRESIDENT

No, but it's not my fault she was kidnapped. This is on you. She was with you when she was taken. It's your job to get her back. Try harder to bring her home.

ANTAL is silent.

DANTE

(angry)

You don't know how much our territory has done to help you! We are here to save you from RAHUMPA. ANTAL is a kind person who is taking time away from his protective duties to find your daughter.

PRESIDENT

ANGELICA was kidnapped because of you. Bring her back.

ANTAL is upset, and they leave the PRESIDENT's office.

ANTAL

I want some time for myself, so please leave me alone. He was missing Angelica every second.

DANTE leaves and calls RAUL to inform him of the current events.

RAUL then talks to ANTAL and tries to motivate him.

ANTAL

(sad)

Hello, Father.

RAUL

I heard you were having a rough time. Are you doing okay?

ANTAL

No, Dad, ANGELICA was kidnapped, and the PRESIDENT is angry that she was with me at the time. He thinks it's my fault and refuses to help me. I miss Angelica more than him. She is love of my life.

RAUL

(sternly)

He is not strong enough to help you. You were there to take care of them. And it's your job to handle all the challenges that come with what you chose to do there. It is your job to help, not to be helped. This is what determines your caliber as a person. Remember these words: Accept this challenge. Whatever happens will be your destiny. So don't worry. Accept it. And prepare yourself for war.

ANTAL

(motivated)

Yes, Dad, you are correct, but I need your army.

RAUL

Keep in mind that you are not an ordinary man.

ANTAL

What do you mean?

RAUL

You could be the king of this territory one day. Carry yourself with pride.

ANTAL

Thanks, Dad, thank you very much.

He hangs up and calls DANTE.

ANTAL

Can you come and take a look at these satellite images?

DANTE

What happened to you? Not long ago, you were really down. But now you look confident.

ANTAL

My father is my role model. He cheered me up and made me realize who I am and who I am meant to be.

DANTE

Why do you want to look at the videos here? Why can't we go to your house?

ANTAL

Who said that? We are not going home.

They use their gadgets to input information about the territories that ANGELICA could be in. Then, they input a photo of ANGELICA through the scan. The computer tries to find her, but it does not find her, but it also shows that there is a region that cannot be seen by this satellite.

ANTAL calls his father.

                              ANTAL

Hi, Dad.

                              RAUL

Hi, son, what happened?

                              ANTAL

Nothing, Dad. I was trying to find the exact location of ANGELICA, but I can't.

                              RAUL

Have you tried your location finder device?

                              ANTAL

Yes, but she's not visible in RAHUMPA's territory, and there is an area that is not viewable.

                              RAUL

Send me her photo. I'll see what I can do.

ANTAL scans her photo and sent it through his goggles by holding a button and commanding it.

RAUL's computer receives the e-mail. RAUL spends hours trying to find ANGELICA.

He calls his son.

RAUL

Hey, son, I haven't gotten the location for ANGELICA. She may be in the same location that is showing as blocked on your device.

ANTAL

Thanks, Dad. Now I know what I need to do

RAUL

What are you going to do now? Come home and prepare yourself for the war, then go looking for ANGELICA?

ANTAL

No, Dad, this time, I will do it by myself.

RAUL

Okay, but if you ever get in trouble, I am here for you.

ANTAL

Thanks, Dad.

He turns to his friend, DANTE.

Raghavendra Rathore and Ramendra Rathor

ANTAL

Is there any way that we could find out where RAHUMPA has taken ANGELICA?

DANTE

I think we can, because when we went to the KING earlier, he saw something by the satellite. I think that I can hack the KING's satellite and can watch what's happening.

ANTAL

Oh! Wow, great! Let's check it out with our own satellite first.

DANTE takes his computer out and starts to work on hacking into the KING's satellite. ANTAL looks at his new gadget.

DANTE

ANTAL! I did it!

(showing ANTAL the screen)

He chose the path that is less visible, but he still passed over a planet known as Saturn.

ANTAL

Do you think that we should go there and check whether they have seen anything or not?

DANTE

Definitely. Let's head there now.

They start the engine and navigation system. Once the plane is off the ground, they receive a radio message.

RADIO

Provide your identity and land your plane. If you don't comply, I will take your plane down myself.

ANTAL

This is ANTAL, son of RAUL. I want to go to the planet Saturn. I am lowering my plane now. Who am I speaking to?

RADIO

Just land your plane and quit asking questions.

Once they land, they look around to find the person who contacted them.

RADIO

Why are you here? This is one of the most secure places in the universe.

ANTAL

(to DANTE)

I studied a lot, but I haven't seen anything about this in my books.

DANTE

Same here, but what should we do?

ANTAL

We are going to Saturn to meet its KING. RAHUMPA kidnapped the PRESIDENT's daughter, ANGELICA. She is my girlfriend, and I am worried about her. I want to know if anyone on Saturn has seen her.

A PERSON steps out of the bushes and puts their radio into their pocket.

PERSON (RADIO)

I am the KING's servant. We are worried about our homeland, because his son, FAVEL, has been in a coma for almost a year. He has been keeping this a secret, because FAVEL has knowledge that no one else in the universe has. FAVEL knows where the keys to the ammunition store-room are. We are trying to be careful.

ANTAL

I see. May we visit him now?

PERSON

Yes.

The PERSON takes ANTAL and DANTE to the throne room. RONITTO is the king now.

ANTAL

We are scientists, and we may be able to cure your son's coma.

RONITTO (KING)

Who is this man?

PERSON

He is the son of RAUL and the prince of RAUL's territory.

RONITTO

Welcome. How can I help you, Prince ANTAL?

ANTAL

My girlfriend, a PRESIDENT's daughter, has been kidnapped by RAHUMPA. I was hoping you could tell me if you saw anyone unfamiliar recently.

RONITTO

Okay, well some the guys seen something 3 days ago in the sky, but we were unable to do anything because my son is in coma stage and he is the only one who knows where he kept all the ammunition store room.

ANTAL

Can I see him?

RONITTO

Oh! Yes, let's head there now.

They head to the meditation room. One nurse is checking FAVEL's blood pressure, and another one is fixing his fluid bags.

They stare at ANTAL. King RONITTO enters the room. The nurses scurry out of the way, check FAVEL's wound dressings, and move to the edge of the room.

ANTAL

I can cure him, but if I do so, then will you help with getting my girlfriend back from RAHUMPA?

RONITTO

Yes, of course. If you can save my son. I miss him dearly.

ANTAL goes to the main room and calls his father.

ANTAL

Hi, Dad, how are you?

RAUL

I am good, but what happened? Is everything all right?

ANTAL

Yes, everything is all right here, but I need the medicine that can cure a comatose patient.

RAUL

Oh! Yes, I do have that. What happened? Is everyone is all right?

ANTAL

Yes, everyone is fine, but I need that for a guy who has been in a coma for almost a year.

RAUL

No problem. It will work. I'll send it right away.

ANTAL

No worries. let know the exact location of the medicine.

RAUL

Okay, it is in the special pharmacy drug store room with department 49, sector 12, and location 56.

ANTAL

Okay, thank you, Dad, once again.

ANTAL puts the address into his special device, and drugs come out to him in only 30 seconds. ANTAL returns to FAVEL's room. He gestures at DANTE to come over. DANTE rolls FAVEL partly onto his side. ANTAL injects the medicine into FAVEL's spinal cord.

ANTAL

Please don't give him any kind of medicine for the next 2 hours.

RONITTO

Okay.

After 1 hour, FAVEL wakes up and comes out of the room and goes to the main hall.

FAVEL

What's going on, Dad? I am very tired and feel like my legs are jammed.

RONITTO

My son, you were in a coma for nearly a year, and due to ANTAL and DANTE, you were able to come out of it.

FAVEL

Thanks! Thank you very much.

FADE TO:

bedroom - evening time

King RONITTO is sitting with his QUEEN.

RONITTO

ANTAL cured our son, but now I am bound to my word. I said I'd help him find his girlfriend.

In the meantime, FAVEL is going through his gate and hears all this. He stops moving and starts listening.

QUEEN

What is the problem with finding his girlfriend?

RONITTO

To help him, we need to go against RAHUMPA, for the sake of my promise. But I don't want to lose our son again.

FAVEL knocks on the door.

RONITTO (CONT'D)

Come in.

FAVEL comes in.

FAVEL

Hey, Dad, I want to ask you something.

RONITTO

What, son? Please speak up.

FAVEL

I heard the conversation between you and Mom. I think you should stick to your promise. You might be afraid of RAHUMPA, but aren't you more afraid of losing me again? This is my second chance at life, and it's all due to ANTAL and DANTE. You should help him. You promised you would.

King RONITTO goes silent, and FAVEL leaves the room.

Morning time

King RONITTO is coming out of his room for breakfast, and his son is already there, as are ANTAL and DANTE.

RONITTO

Welcome, Mr. ANTAL, have you gotten good sleep?

ANTAL

Yes, sir.

RONITTO

So do you have any plans to search for your girlfriend?

ANTAL

I know the direction that where I need to go, but I haven't planned anything like that.

RONITTO

Well, in my opinion, you should plan everything. This is GERALD, who will be the commanding officer for you from my army.

ANTAL

Thank you.

FAVEL

I will go with him.

RONITTO

But you are weak. I am not trying to stop you to go and help him, but first be strong enough to help him.

But at the same times he stand up and says you want to see how good am I, let see how fast I can run and I can jump,

But after two rounds of the ground, he faints.

ANTAL

Get some water!

And a PERSON gets some water, ANTAL put some drops of water on FAVEL's face, and he wakes up.

FAVEL

I am sorry, Mr. ANTAL. My Dad is correct; I need some rest to be like I was before.

ANTAL

No problem. I can understand your feelings.

CUT TO:

Planet view:

ANTAL gets his army and starts to move forward. He goes over the planet where RAHUMPA fights with a PERSON before taking ANGELICA into his territory.

RAHUMPA'S SON, SATUSTA has become a leader of army. He looks through the telescope and sees a very big army going towards RAHUMPA's territory. They keep moving, and he keeps watching.

ANTAL

Should we ask this planet's people whether they have seen anything or not?

DANTE

Now we need not to ask anything to anyone; we know who did that.

ANTAL

Ohhh!!! Yes, let's move.

They reach the front of the planet of RAHUMPA's territory, and they see that there is something that surrounds the planet. To confirm that, they fire a small round towards it, but it cannot pass through the transparent, shining, blue light around the planet, while all RAHUMPA's people get an alert about the attempt.

An army approaches ANTAL and his army.

ANTAL

(Frightened)

Pull back, pull back! Something is coming! Pull back!

(Worried)

Those things could strike some of the planes! Those are actually small missiles and will destroy whatever they hit.

FADE TO:

EXTRA-TERRESTRIAL PLANET

The PLANET'S KING is watching this destruction through his telescope.

He calls his personal aid.

PLANET'S KING

Send a message to that army and ask them to pull back as much as can and ask them to come to my planet. They may stay here for a time.

His personal aid sends the message, and ANTAL, with his entire army, comes there to hide from RAHUMPA's missiles.

ANTAL lets all the army rest there and goes to the PLANET'S KING's room with his friend.

ANTAL

Thank you so much for letting us rest here, King BASHIN.

BASHIN (planet's KING)

By the way, who are you? And why do you want to be in trouble by fighting with RAHUMPA? It won't end well.

ANTAL

I am a prince of RAUL's territory, and RAHUMPA kidnapped my girlfriend, and we are here to go to war with him.

BASHIN

That's okay, but what's the problem with entering his territory?

ANTAL

There is a shield covering the planet. It does not allow anything to get inside the atmosphere.

BASHIN

Let me see the satellite view in slow motion.

BASHIN sees that when they throw a stone on it, it pulses but gives the two sides of waves.

BASHIN (CONT'D)
It is more or less the same thing that we have.

ANTAL
What?

BASHIN
We have the same technology to protect ourselves. Now I am going to do what RAHUMPA did to protect himself from us.

ANTAL
You have an answer to it?

BASHIN
I have a pipe that can expand in size. I am going to cover it with electromagnetic waves so that it will easily accept the electromagnetic waves of that planet, and after that, we can easily enter the territory.

ANTAL
I have a question for you.

BASHIN

Do you want to know why I am trying to help you?

ANTAL

Yes, because no one wants to fight with RAHUMPA, and you are helping us, and you also want to get involved in it. Why? I am not getting that.

BASHIN

Because when RAHUMPA was trying to escape after kidnapping your girlfriend, he went this way, and my father protested against him and was killed.

DANTE

So he has gone through this way?

BASHIN

Yes.

ANTAL

So do you know where he's taken her?

BASHIN

(sadly)

I don't know, because his plane is so fast that I cannot see it. Because my father died, I was so sad that I didn't want to look after that.

ANTAL

I am sorry about that.

BASHIN

It's okay. I am all right. I have to be strong like my father was.

ANTAL

I don't think that a smart guy like RAHUMPA is going to trust only a shield; he may have something else as well for security.

BASHIN looks at a satellite view for himself, and three different PEOPLE are always watching it from different locations.

ANTAL

How do we stop it? By endorsing a virus and letting the frame repeat for every 30 minutes.

BASHIN

Let's give it a try.

ANTAL uses the same technology to bring the virus to space. Three jet planes are securing the satellite, but ANTAL and DANTE kill all three at the time so they would not be able to send any reports to RAHUMPA. They reach the satellite and input the virus into its software. DANTE reports to BASHIN that it has been installed, and he and ANTAL move very fastback to BASHIN.

Here, BASHIN already is with his army to the front of the planet. ANTAL reaches there.

BASHIN

I was waiting for you.

ANTAL

I think we'll be safe this time.

BASHIN

Perfect. I even found a place with almost no population.

ANTAL

Okay, let's go.

BASHIN enters the pipe, and slowly, slowly adjusts it so that it will not create any waves. The size of the pipe increases, for they need to enter the measurements into the computer. Then, all the army enters the region of the planet, and finally, ANTAL and BASHIN enter.

Cut to:

RAHUMPA'S TERRITORY SUPERCOMPUTER ROOM

Two PEOPLE at RAHUMPA's territory notice that something is wrong with the video feeds today.

PERSON #1

What happened?

PERSON #2

Because I can see that the same guy comes to a shop, then leaves and comes back to the shop, and then he leaves again and repeats this process over and over. This has been going on for the last four hours.

PERSON #1

That's weird.

PERSON #2

What could it be? Check it with another satellite on top of this one.

FADE OUT.

ANTAL and BASHIN enter the region

FADE OUT.

RAHUMPA'S TERRITORY SUPERCOMPUTER PLACE

PERSON #1 pulls up another satellite and sees some kind of black thing from space to territory and calls PERSON #2 to verify something on their screen.

PERSON #2

I think you should check your eyes.

PERSON #1

Why?

PERSON #2

Because there is nothing.

PERSON #1

Let me see. Oh, yes, there is nothing. Maybe I was dreaming. Thanks.

PERSON #2

All right, no problem.

PERSON #1

But there is something wrong with the satellite computer, because it is showing something different from the other satellite.

PERSON #2

It happens Sometimes. Fix it.

PERSON #1

Okay.

PERSON #1 fixes it.

CUT TO:

ANTAL'S ARMY ENTERING

ANTAL and his whole army enter RAHUMPA's territory and set up a workstation and set down a projector that reflects all the images on the roof of the workstation. It shows the heat signatures and warns of activity and high speeds.

ANTAL

We don't know that where ANGELICA is and I think that she must be getting worried about herself that whether someone is going to come and help her.

BASHIN is silent, but GERALD comes in.

GERALD

I have a guy who can do this job very well. He is a very intelligent and tactful person.

ANTAL

Who is he?

GERALD

He is the same guy who will take you to the king and let you have a treaty to work together. He is named GELANDO.

ANTAL

Call him here right now.

He calls for GELANDO, who walks over.

ANTAL

Hi, GELANDO, how are you?

GELANDO

I am very good, sir. How can I help you?

ANTAL

I want to send a message to my girlfriend, saying that I am coming to help her and that there is no need to worry.

GELANDO

Okay, sir, I think I can do that, but there will be the issue of RAHUMPA's high security.

ANTAL

For that, I am giving you a gadget that will let you disguise yourself, to look like anyone's face and go anywhere. Here is the other gadget. With it, you can create a view anywhere so that no one will be able to know what's going on the other side, and it is really fast.

GELANDO

This is all good, but how do I convince her that I'm with you, not RAHUMPA?

ANTAL

Well, I have one thing. She gifted to me this shirt; my and her names are written on this shirt. That's all I have.

GELANDO

I think it should work.

ANTAL

My goal is to calm her down, okay?

GELANDO

Okay.

GELANDO moves to meet ANGELICA and gets closer to the populated area. When he was going from there, he sees a PERSON who leaves their house. By the side of that house, he waits for 5 minutes and then takes a picture and starts to move.

But when he starts to move, a high-class LADY comes over to him.

LADY

Well, you are so lazy! I know that you would not be able to leave this street so quickly!

GELANDO

Oh! Sorry!

LADY

This time, it is good that you came back, because I forgot to give you this bag. Take it and leave, and please try to go quickly for once.

GELANDO

Oh, yeah, sure.

Then the LADY moves into the house.

GELANDO

I am leaving.

GELANDO leaves from there and is wearing his glasses too high, examining the map of where he needs to go.

LADY

Now where are you going?

GELANDO

What happened? I have the bag and am trying to move faster.

LADY

The market is that way, not this way.

GELANDO

Ohhh! Well, I was testing you, to see whether you know the way to the market or not.

LADY

I go to the market all the time, not you, okay?

He starts to move to the direction of the LADY.

She moves off the pathway, and GELANDO sees a new person and takes the face of that person. He comes back from the same way, and the LADY is still there. When GELANDO sees her, he gets frightened and stops moving.

LADY

Hey, you, why are you staring at me like that?

GELANDO

Noooo, it's not like that. I am going on my way.

LADY

Wait a minute. You have my husband's bag.

GELANDO

No, no, no, this is not mine. I found it on the street and picked it up.

LADY

No, you are a thief, and you have stolen my husband's bag.

GELANDO (V.O.)

Oh my god, what is her problem? Please leave me alone!

GELANDO

No, nothing is like that, but if you still want this bag, you can keep it.

He hands over her bag and hops into a nearby taxi.

CUT TO:

GELANDO reaches a location closer where ANGELICA is being kept.

GELANDO

Is this Belindo Street?

PERSON

Yes.

GELANDO goes to the place where he found a guard who finished his duty hours and going back to his home. He follows him and finds a place that is secret. This time, the guard is in the car, so he strikes him from the back, but his car is very safe and he doesn't get hurt.

GUARD #1

What are you doing?

GELANDO shoots him and kills him, and then he puts his dead body into his car and tosses it from a mountain.

In the morning, he comes to the same place, scans his badge, and goes inside, and he takes the picture out of his pocket and tries to match it with some of the ladies, and finally, he finds her and tries to go inside her prison.

GUARD #2

Hey, where are you going?

GELANDO

I'm looking inside.

GUARD #2

Don't you know that it is not allowed?

GELANDO

Oh! Okay.

GELANDO stops doing anything and waits and wait, until the time he goes for toilet, and when he goes, he starts his gadget, hiding him from sight.

He comes to his real posture and goes close to ANGELICA, but she gets scared and is about to scream, but he shows her the shirt ANTAL gave him.

GELANDO

Please don't scream; I was sent by Mr. ANTAL. I am here to say please don't worry and we have come here to get you out of this place.

ANGELICA

But they are very powerful, and I don't think that anyone can fight with RAHUMPA.

GELANDO

No, nothing is like that, I think you don't know the power of Mr. ANTAL.

ANGELICA

Even my father has refused to go for a war, so whom should I believe?

GELANDO

You should believe in Mr. ANTAL and our army.

But ANGELICA is still looking depressed.

GELANDO

Look, ma'am, look at me.

Then GELANDO takes his shirt off to show that he is powerful. He takes his computer out and hacked into the computer of RAHUMPA.

GELANDO

Here are all the cameras of this city. You want to see them?

He takes out his gadget and dials ANTAL. ANTAL answers, and his image show up.

ANTAL

Hi, ANGELICA, don't worry. I am here, and you will be free very soon.

ANGELICA

Oh! (Sad and crying) RAHUMPA told me that my father has refused to come releasing me. I was so depressed, but I have faith in you; I love you so much.

ANTAL

Don't worry and be quiet; do not let anyone know that we have reached here

GELANDO puts his gadget back into his pocket.

GELANDO

Don't worry, I will back, but next time, I will be with Mr. ANTAL. See you soon.

ANGELICA

Okay, bye.

He takes all the stuff back and starts to move from there, but an OFFICER approaches him.

OFFICER

Who are you?

And GELANDO tries to look at his name badge and say the name.

OFFICER

Do you know where her office is?

GELANDO

No.

OFFICER

She should be your wife, but you are not that person, because the person you look like was found dead. Guards, seize him!

All the guards approach to him and at the same time he explode a small bomb that create a smoke and he get lost from there and he took the mask of that officer this time, but all the guards have the report that GELANDO is coming from this exit. When he comes out, all the guards approach him again.

OFFICER

What are you doing here, standing idly?

GUARD

Sir we have the information that he is coming from this exit.

GELANDO

Yes, he was coming from this exit, but when I tried to approach him, he left to the 13B exit gate.

But the real officer comes to there.

OFFICER

What are you doing, fools? He is the guy; catch him!

GELANDO runs again, and this time, OFFICER comes close to him, and they have a little fight. The guards arrive and catch GELANDO, and they take him to the interrogation room in the prison.

CUT TO:

Int. RAHUMPA's office

INFORMANT

Someone has entered our territory. It is a man of six foot, with black hair, and has lot of powers. He spoke with ANGELICA, but he was caught after a hot pursuit.

RAHUMPA to his son Satusta

He must be a guy of ANTAL. Son, you should go and find more details.

And then both of them take his car and flee to the interrogation room.

SATUSTA

(Aggressively)

How dare you enter our territory and try to fly away without any welcome?

SATUSTA

Now tell me what your plan is. If you tell me, I can let you go. Otherwise, maybe I won't.

GELANDO

No, I am not that guy, believe me! I can prove it if you set me free first.

SATUSTA

Okay, let him free.

GELANDO

Sir, he is very fast, and if you set him free, then he will try to run away.

SATUSTA

Let him loose. I am here. He's not going anywhere.

He lets him free, and that PERSON takes his hand to his shoulder and gets a gadget out, and his body changes to a PERSON who works as a chief of prisoners over there.

All of them get shocked and SATUSTA takes his gun out and is about to shoot him, but RAHUMPA stops him.

RAHUMPA

Don't waste your energy like this; use it constructively and go look for him at the satellite, then let me know.

SATUSTA

As you said.

FADE TO:

Ext. ANTAL's tent

GELANDO is running as fast as he can to ANTAL's station.

ANTAL

Hi, GELANDO, are you all right?

GELANDO

Yes, sir, I am quite good, by the grace of god.

ANTAL

That's good, but I was watching everything and saw that you got caught by the officer.

GELANDO (V.O. WITH FLASHBACK)

No, sir, actually, when he was coming closer to me, we had a small fight. Then I changed to look like the officer and ran away. I was too fast for them.

GERALD

I am happy that you got here in time.

GELANDO

I find that the sun over here is up for 9 hours, and you know that our power decreases after the sunsets.

ANTAL

Really? My god, why didn't you tell me about that earlier?

GERALD

I forgot, because we have a sun all the time on our planet.

FADE IN:

ANTAL goes to BASHIN.

ANTAL

Hi, King BASHIN, how is it going?

BASHIN

Good. What happened?

ANTAL

Well, I found out that GERALD and his team cannot live without sunlight. Do you have anything to work with that?

BASHIN

Well, no, but I still request you to come with me.

On the way, he reaches his army battalion and calls one of them to the front.

BASHIN

Now I request you to take your most powerful weapon and hit him.

ANTAL

Why?

BASHIN

Do as I am saying.

ANTAL

Okay.

Then ANTAL takes his missile and hits him directly, and there is nothing left, and both of them can see little bubbles on the ground.

ANTAL

What is that?

BASHIN

This army is all about the robots and this army cannot die! They look like us, but it is not like us, ha-ha!

ANTAL

Thanks for being with me, ha-ha!

FADE TO:

At the lab, all the satellite maps can be seen there and son of RAHUMPA reaches there.

SATUSTA

Hey, have you seen anything that tried to enter our territory?

PEOPLE

No, what happened?

SATUSTA

Unfortunately swine enters our territory under your nose and meets the prisoner ANGELICA and running back to somewhere in our territory.

SATUSTA

I want that you guys search every corner of our territory and let me know where that guy is.

All the PEOPLE get busy in searching every corner of the territory, and one person can see some kind of clouds at one place and tried to figure it out, but it was quite impossible. The person sends all this information to SATUSTA by making a file of pictures with his report.

SATUSTA takes them to RAHUMPA.

RAHUMPA

They are right here.

SATUSTA

I also think so, but I'm not so sure.

RAHUMPA

Don't be unsure. They are hiding at that place in our territory. Get ready for war.

And then SATUSTA officially announces the war to the soldiers.

Int. meeting hall - evening

SATUSTA, RAHUMPA, and his four-army heads are sitting in the meeting hall, and RAHUMPA is leading the meeting

RAHUMPA

(Aggressive) (Pointing towards the map)

As you guys can see, this part of the map is dominantly covered by clouds. I am very sure our enemy is trying to hide there.

PERSON

How did he enter our territory?

RAHUMPA

How does that matter? But the thing is that tomorrow we are
going to attack them.

RAHUMPA

(pointing towards one person)

By tomorrow morning, you start to attack at the very center of
the clouds through missiles.

(now pointing towards another person)

At the same time you two will keep your all the armed forces
ready to attack from the ground (pointing towards the son) you
will be with me at my lab by this morning and have to tell me
every small thing going on there and be prepared yourself for
the air attack.

SATUSTA

Why shouldn't we attack with whole strength at once?

RAHUMPA

Because maybe he is ready for us, and I want to know how much
he knows.

RAHUMPA

Any more questions?

ALL THE PEOPLE

No, sir.

Int. Laboratory - day

RAHUMPA with SATUSTA, in laboratory talking to a team head.

RAHUMPA

Are you ready to attack?

PERSON

Yes, sir.

RAHUMPA

What about you guys?

ALL THE PEOPLE

We all are ready.

CUT TO:

Int. ANTAL's tent - day

All the people are sleeping, but his scientists are working.

FADE OUT.

Int. Laboratory - day

RAHUMPA orders to fire the missile.

And the missile gets fired.

RAHUMPA and all his team heads and everyone are watching the screen.

FADE IN:

Int. ANTAL's tent - day

An alarm starts instantly, and ANTAL and all his team heads wake up and see that something having heat in it is reaching their tent very quickly.

ANTAL acts very fast and pushes the emergency button that makes a noise to wake up all the army.

Screen shows on the roof auto-defense and fire starts to show a map on the screen and tracks the missile and launches another missile towards it and destroys it before it reaches ANTAL's tent.

Everyone is afraid.

ANTAL

(Aggressively)

Go outside and tell everyone that war is on and be prepared for commands. Get in a line. The war is on and be prepared for the war and wait for our command for our move.

BASHIN activates all his army too and sets them all for war and taking commands.

FADE OUT.

Int. Laboratory - day

RAHUMPA

Shit!

The team heads are shocked.

RAHUMPA

Computer, what's happening there?

COMPUTER

They are using technology as auto-defenses.

RAHUMPA

Okay, but they cannot carry this many missiles and ammunition with them.

COMPUTER

Yes, they are not doing that, but they are simply transporting them all from their home lab.

RAHUMPA

Is there any loophole for that?

COMPUTER

Let me see.

Then the COMPUTER turns on a little music.

COMPUTER

They have missile launchers. It takes 30 seconds for one to get transported to them.

RAHUMPA

Thanks, Computer. Everyone, stop all the firing for 2 minutes.

CUT TO:

ANTAL's tent

All the firing stops, and ANTAL's army shouts and cheers.

FADE OUT.

RAHUMPA'S BATTLEFIELD

They launch 10 missiles towards the main camp station.

All the missiles launch and they are reaching the lab center. There are lights flashing.

The signal starts beeping.

ANTAL

(in a hurry)

Now leave this place; it is going to experience a very severe attack now.

All start to run to new places and gather there.

A small blast sound comes, and all the people look at the lab and see that all the launch pads detached with the station and landed on the ground far enough away that no one got hurt.

Ten missiles blast on the lab, and huge blast occur, and RAHUMPA is very unhappy.

RAHUMPA

(angrily)

Attack them again.

The army head releases all the army to attack ANTAL's army.

RAHUMPA's army is coming with huge sounds and firing with guns and tanks.

BASHIN reaches ANTAL.

BASHIN

Let me charge my army.

ANTAL nods his head.

And BASHIN's army goes on attack while ANTAL calls GELANDO to him.

ANTAL

Just send your five best people to this location.

(showing them on a gadget)

Because this is the command station. Destroy it.

And GELANDO send GERALD and four other people escape from the army and head to the station.

FADE TO:

Ext. Battlefield - morning

Both the armies are firing at each other. Bullets go to BASHIN's army and hit them. It does not harm them; they pass out, and then they get healed again, but RAHUMPA's army gets injured with the bullets.

COMMANDER

Let's get the artillery to do the job and blast them.

When the bombs attack them, BASHIN's army gets small drops and then recollects them and are again ready to attack.

COMMANDER

Hide yourself and keep firing.

And the whole army hides themselves and keeps firing.

CUT TO:

Int. Laboratory - morning

RAHUMPA is very shocked and signals his son to attack from the sky with a secret weapon: a robo-spider.

RAHUMPA

(shouting)

Son, attack them right now from sky and give the answer of machine with the machine.

And now his son goes with all the army to attack from the sky and releases his missile on them. The missile explodes, and small robotic spiders come out of it. They move toward BASHIN's army.

SATUSTA releases some other missiles at BASHIN's army that scattered BASHIN's army and small droplet have been formed due to the blast and then all the spiders come to action.

They reach every drop and make a bubble with their mouth and pack every bubble so that they cannot rearrange themselves and get collected.

FADE OUT.

Int. laboratory - afternoon

RAHUMPA

Computer, release a missile with the nitrogen on them so that it will stabilize the electrons of those machines. And after that, release my army that does the same thing.

RAHUMPA has the same kind of army, but his army does not require rearranging itself, because it is modified so that each droplet is one person.

RAHUMPA's army goes into the war and makes a huge damage.

ANTAL is not having any answer to it and calls his father.

ANTAL

Oh! Father, RAHUMPA has killed all BASHIN's army, the ones that I thought that can never be killed, and now he has released the same army, but it is a more advanced one.

RAUL takes a look.

RAUL

My son, the only way you can destroy them is to burn them when they are unstable. They are unstable at the transition time when they are coming down to earth.

ANTAL hangs up the phone and gets into the real action.

He gets the missile and fires at them, and then uses his flamethrower and gun stabilizer.

RAHUMPA

What's going on there? call my army back!

And then RAHUMPA get all the army back and command for a sky attachment with all the power, and ANTAL asks his army to go in the sky and ready for war.

War is very dense and both the parties are doing very well, and damage can be seen at both sides.

FADE TO:

Int. RAHUMPA's office - afternoon

RAHUMPA and his son are looking very angry and worried.

SATUSTA

Father, why don't you put down the spider web?

RAHUMPA

Because ANTAL knows how to break it.

SATUSTA

But no one else does.

RAHUMPA

But they all know it now.

SATUSTA

Father, I will set up the station with that in a certain field they will be transition of ammunition.

RAHUMPA

Okay, but ANTAL--

SATUSTA

I will take him away.

He starts to move toward ANTAL's army.

This time, camera takes the pic from the lower part of the spiral formed by RAHUMPA and moving towards ANTAL's army

ANTAL is not there because SATUSTA has already taken him away from here, they are engaged in a blasting fight.

The people are forming a spiral. There is an army head with a special plane, and at the end of it, RAHUMPA is standing with four of his main army heads; there is an antiaircraft gun type at the center so that no one will be able to come from the bottom to the top of the spiral.

DANTE

(To BASHIN)

What is this and how can we answer it?

BASHIN

This is a spiral and I think he is going to start a spiral war. I don't know how to answer it.

DANTE looks at it.

DANTE

Let me have a satellite view of it.

He looks at it.

DANTE

I think it would be really easy. All we need to drop a nice bomb at the middle of the spiral.

BASHIN

Let's try it.

And then DANTE sends his one of the best people from his army, who goes there and drops the bomb.

RAHUMPA sees that on his screen and gives the signal to his person.

Two missiles launch from the center of the spiral and go so fast that ANTAL's person has released the bomb. One missile attacks the bomb, and another missile attacks his plane. And the spiral continues to move forward in a slow motion.

DANTE and all others get so shocked by seeing RAHUMPA's technology and good missiles, and DANTE moves to his plane.

His ammunition will never be enough. He calls his whole army to ready themselves for war, and BASHIN reaches there.

BASHIN

Sir, what I learned from the satellite view is that RAHUMPA has installed a transition jammer. It means that your ammunition will not be available to you inside the spiral.

DANTE stops.

DANTE

(upset)

Then what to do? We have to do something; otherwise, they will hit our main station.

(beat)

Load as much ammunition as you can in your plane and get ready for my signal, and we will go in a straight line. Any questions?

SOLDIERS

No, sir.

DANTE

I will lead you this time.

And DANTE goes for the war without ANTAL, and all the PEOPLE follow him into battle.

Camera takes a look from the far side, showing a straight line trying to go into the spiral.

DANTE launches his first very powerful missile; all the PEOPLE of RAHUMPA comes in that range get in to the particles, and the army going with him launches the fire weapon so that all the particles get burned at the same time.

This way, he breaks the first line of the spiral and 50% of the army that he brought with him gets in the spiral's first circle. The second level will send reinforcements to the first circle to stop the incoming army. The army head of that circle moves to downward to make another circle more difficult.

And then he uses the same thing and enters into the third circle.

DANTE enters into the circle with 10% of his army, and again, both the army heads move to the inner circle and reinforcement heads from the inner circle to the outer circle to stop more incoming enemies.

And DANTE looks at his army and gets worried by seeing very few of them with him and realizes that he made a mistake, but he has no choice and again does the same thing to enter one more circle, but this time, he pages ANTAL to get back as soon as possible and launches a camera in the sky so that ANTAL would not make the same mistake.

CUT TO:

Int. ANTAL's plane

ANTAL gets the message from his friend and realizes that this chase is nothing but a trap to keep him away from his army, and he starts to move very fast to his army.

FADE TO:

DANTE's plane

DANTE enters the innermost circle alone with his one of his helpers.

DANTE is left with very little ammunition.

DANTE

Are you okay?

PERSON

I am all right.

A sound of blast can be heard, and he looks around.

His helper is dead. He was shot by one of RAHUMPA's troops. DANTE turns around his plane to give him the answer and fire back, but his missile has been destroyed. DANTE fires another missile and hits one of RAHUMPA's soldiers.

Then DANTE fires another missile at another person.

DANTE hears a ticking sound and looks at the screen. It displays that he has no more missiles.

DANTE

Hey, ANTAL, I am out of ammo.

DANTE tries to reach to the transmission jammer device to destroy it.

Another sound of a blast comes.

DANTE gets a very big shake in his plane and sees one the screen that one side of his plane has been destroyed and that another missile is coming from another side.

This time, he moves his plane to another side, but it is difficult. He dodges it, but the missile destroys the jammer device for him.

DANTE feels a little bit happy, but he pushes the button to escape from the plane. Once on land, he takes out his laser beam sword to defend himself from some of the firing coming from RAHUMPA's troops.

But a bullet hits his sword and his sword flies out of his hand.

Then RAHUMPA and few of this army heads start to laugh at him and fire their guns.

RAHUMPA

Are you scared? Well, I can leave you, but then you'd have to fight by my side.

And again, he starts to laugh.

DANTE feels humiliated and runs toward his plane.

He pulls the fan off his destroyed plane and throws it toward RAHUMPA.

Someone blocks RAHUMPA and takes the hit for him.

And then all of RAHUMPA's troops, along with RAHUMPA, reach DANTE and kill him with their laser swords.

CUT TO:

Ext. Battlefield - day

ANTAL is trying to reach there as soon as possible and is watching everything inside his plane. He feels awful about that and gets very angry and starts to run towards that place.

SATUSTA starts to follow him and messages RAHUMPA to say that ANTAL is coming towards him.

CUT TO:

Ext. Battlefield - day

RAHUMPA gets the information from his son and sends it to all his army heads

RAHUMPA

Just get yourself rearranged for another victory.

All the army heads try to rearrange the army.

RAHUMPA gives the direction to his army to move towards ANTAL's army and attack them again.

CUT TO:

Ext. Battlefield - day

ANTAL puts his plane on autopilot and watches the video from the satellite. He sees his friend DANTE die with honor.

His plane reaches their station, and he runs to his fellow troops.

PEOPLE

(Gathering around ANTAL and weeping)

We were not able to save your friend.

PERSON

They are again planning to attack us with same strategy.

ANTAL

(Angry)

Let's prepare for the war, and this time, we are going to teach a lesson to them and get revenge for my friend's death.

All of them cheer ANTAL and his army. This time, ANTAL arrives and pulls out one of the most powerful missiles and targets it towards RAHUMPA's army, then fires it.

He fires everywhere, and RAHUMPA's army starts to die off. ANTAL kills them in the circles of the spiral. ANTAL's army gets inside the spiral, along with ANTAL.

GERALD and his army are on very small plane that moves fast and does a lot of damage to RAHUMPA's army.

This makes it quite impossible for RAHUMPA's army heads to get back into the inner circle.

CUT TO:

Ext. Battlefield – day

SATUSTA has seen everything and is furious.

SATUSTA

COMPUTER, who are they, and what is their weakness?

The COMPUTER takes a second.

COMPUTER

They are from Saturn, and that planet has the sunlight all the time. That's why these people cannot live for long without sunlight.

RAHUMPA'S SON looks at the computer and understands the implications.

SATUSTA

COMPUTER, release half of the army to stand in the front of the sun and cover all the sunlight of the battlefield and defend them from any weapon.

FADE TO:

Ext. Battlefield - day

All the machines and ANTAL's army are fighting, and machines are getting destroyed. ANTAL fires a bullet towards a machine but misses the shot because those machines start to fly into the sky.

ANTAL is surprised and confused about what's going on.

BASHIN

Come to ANTAL. I think that they are running from us! We might have won the war! Hurry!

ANTAL smiles, and BASHIN falls unconscious.

ANTAL tries to wake him, and then calls GERALD to come help.

ANTAL sees all the people on the ground from BASHIN's army.

ANTAL sees all the rest of RAHUMPA's army start to point their ammunition towards ANTAL.

ANTAL gets on his plane, and RAHUMPA's army starts to fire towards ANTAL.

ANTAL sees something in the sky.

BASHIN and his army are unconscious because the sun is being eclipsed by the machines and planes.

ANTAL points his most powerful weapons towards those machines. A missile is going towards it, but it explodes.

SATUSTA launches a very good missile towards ANTAL, and ANTAL has no chance to defend himself.

A huge blast occurs.

The screen goes black and flips twice from black to white.

The PRESIDENT arrives with an army and gives ANTAL a new plane.

PRESIDENT

You can't take over him so easily. The girl who was kidnapped is my daughter. I am going to fight for her, ANTAL.

ANTAL

Let me get BASHIN's army first.

He releases plenty of missiles towards those machines, but nothing happens. All of them had already been destroyed by those machines.

SATUSTA releases some of his missiles towards ANTAL.

ANTAL runs from the missiles and destroys them by focusing them on the parabolic path and clicking on the missile, just as his father taught him to.

All the missiles get destroyed, and he passes by a planet and gets some light, but there is no sun.

It is a reflection of the moon.

ANTAL

Computer, give me any kind of missile that can reflect light.

The computer gives him a crystal-making missile bomb, and ANTAL launches it.

That missile goes into the space and forms a crystal that starts to reflect the light.

BASHIN and his army and ANTAL are feeling somewhat happy, but a sound comes.

His crystal is being destroyed by SATUSTA.

ANTAL tells the PRESIDENT to command his army to release a missile towards the sun at the count of 10.

The PRESIDENT does the same thing as they release their missiles at the same time.

There are many crystals in the sky, and they start to give a beautiful reflection of light onto the battlefield.

SATUSTA starts to destroy the crystals and has his machine do the same.

ANTAL gets to SATUSTA and connects himself to his computer.

ANTAL

(smugly)

Happy birthday!

ANTAL releases a missile towards him and destroys the plane.

RAHUMPA sees that ANTAL killed SATUSTA. He is so angry that he comes to the battlefield and connects himself to the PRESIDENT's computer and ANTAL's computer.

RAHUMPA

(angry)

You guys have made a big mistake.

RAHUMPA pulls out a huge machine through his transportation system.

RAHUMPA

I think that this is the time to clean all this mess up from here.

RAHUMPA starts his machine, and it starts to suck everything in.

RAHUMPA, for the very first time, points towards PRESIDENT's army. Almost 70% of their army has been sucked in.

They start to run to save themselves. RAHUMPA points it towards ANTAL, who starts to run towards the big meteors. The machine is sucking all the meteors coming in the way, and ANTAL turns it towards a different black hole and keeps running towards another black hole. The machine goes towards the black hole, and black hole sucks in the sucking machine.

ANTAL moves towards RAHUMPA and releases a missile towards RAHUMPA.

RAHUMPA's plane gets destroyed, but RAHUMPA gets his jetpack and jumps out of the plane.

RAHUMPA takes out his sword and invites ANTAL and all of them to fight.

First, the PRESIDENT goes for it.

They are fighting with laser swords, but RAHUMPA is dominating the situation and is about to kill him.

ANTAL puts his sword in the front of RAHUMPA's sword to protect ANGELICA's father, but RAHUMPA pushes a button on his sword and extends it, killing the PRESIDENT.

RAHUMPA

(proudly)

No one can save my enemy from me.

And now ANTAL and RAHUMPA are having a good fight. ANTAL got hit on his arm a little bit. The army is shocked.

ANTAL hits RAHUMPA on his leg and then on his right arm, but they are very little scratches because RAHUMPA's sword has an aura that acts as a protecting shield around RAHUMPA.

ANTAL hits the thumb of RAHUMPA.

RAHUMPA loses his sword and ANTAL is about to kill him.

RAHUMPA starts to laugh and ANTAL stops.

RAHUMPA

(laughing)

You have already lost the war, because I already killed ANGELICA.

ANTAL

(angry)

No, it is not possible!

RAHUMPA

If you think so, then check this out.

RAHUMPA shows him a video of ANGELICA's death.

ANTAL is shocked and sad, but he hears ANGELICA not too far away, calling his name.

She was able to escaped and fighting to join ANTAL.

RAHUMPA gets his sword back and is almost there to kill ANTAL, but BASHIN has come in between ANTAL and RAHUMPA. He dies next to ANTAL.

RAHUMPA attacks back, but this time, ANTAL hold the hands of RAHUMPA and turns the sword towards RAHUMPA with the same speed as RAHUMPA coming to kill him.

RAHUMPA's sword is about to penetrates RAHUMPA, but Mahumpa came in between, and Mehar cried. He is your brother, Mahumpa told ANTAL before dying.

Mehar (he is your brother, you have same father) stop this war.

Rahumpa: its too late mom. I must win this war, no matter what?

ANATAL FIRED MISSILES TO RAHUMPA

HE GETS KILLED, BUT ANOTHER ONE COMES AFTER FIRST ONE DIED.

MEHAR: YOU CANT KILL HIM.

ANTAL: I DON'T WANT TO, BUT TO PEACE FOR ALL I WILL DESTROY SUPERCOMPUTER, FOR MAKING ILLUSION.

A BIG BLAST DESTROYED SUPERLAB OF RAHUMPA.

AND HE COMES TO ATTACK HIM FROM BEHIND, BUT GOT KILLED FROM HIS MOTHER MEHAR. I CAN'T LET THIS GROW ANY MORE. I CAN'T DO THIS. (ANATAL speaks to Mehar, and told her, you have saved all kind of humanity and from now he will be like your son.)

All of them are happy about winning the war, but they are sad about losing ANGELICA's father, BASHIN, DANTE, and some other good people.

GERALD

ANTAL, destroy RAHUMPA's planet. There are many other labs that were running via RAHUMPA's technology. If someone else gets to them, it would be dangerous for all of us.

ANTAL

Yes, you are right.

(turning to the general)

It's time. Destroy all their labs.

ANTAL kisses ANGELICA.

***** THE END *****

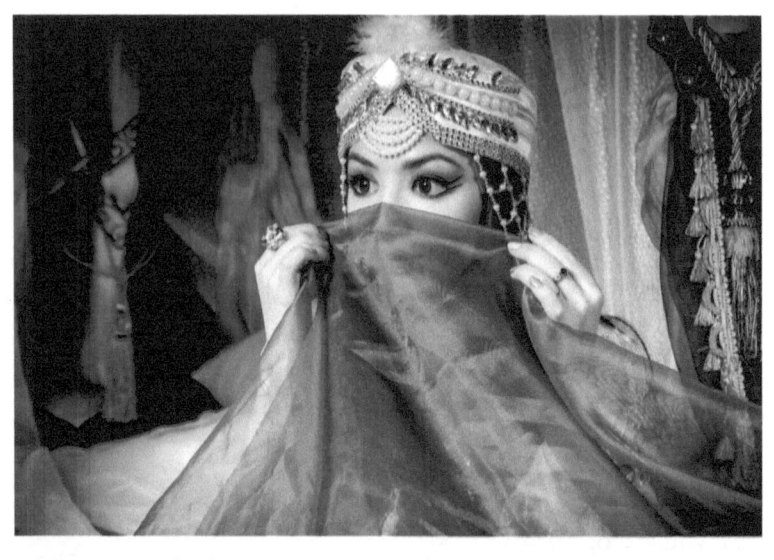

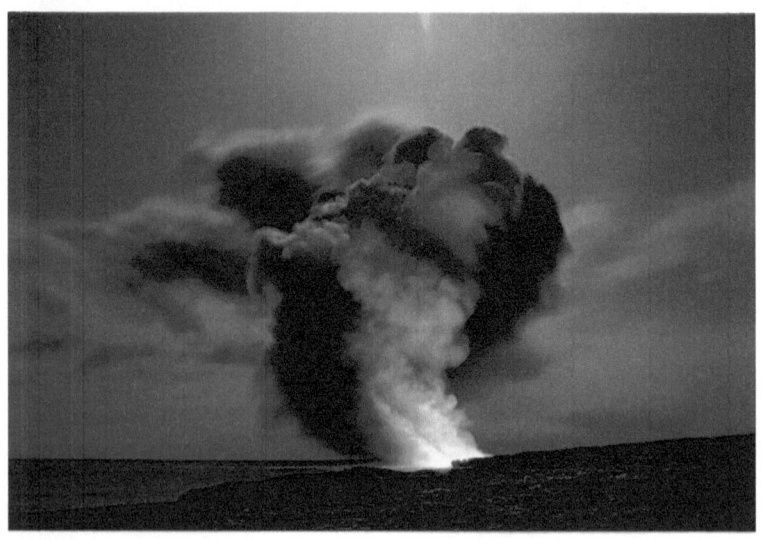

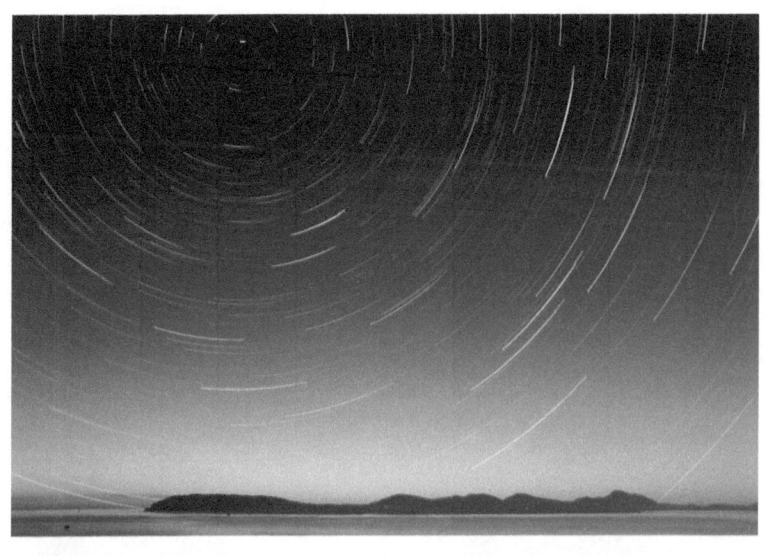

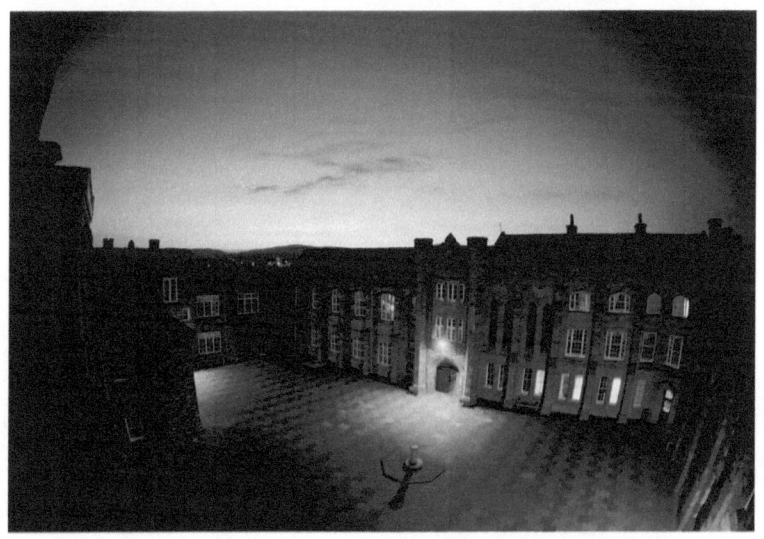

www.ingramcontent.com/pod-product-compliance
Lightning Source LLC
Chambersburg PA
CBHW020917180526
45163CB00007B/2767